D1558059

LIGHT AND COLOR

CONNECTING STUDENTS TO SCIENCE SERIES

By
DR. BARBARA R. SANDALL

COPYRIGHT © 2003 Mark Twain Media, Inc.

ISBN 1-58037-250-3

Printing No. CD-1613

Mark Twain Media, Inc., Publishers
Distributed by Carson-Dellosa Publishing Company, Inc.

TABLE OF CONTENTS

INTRODUCTION TO THE SERIES

The Connecting Students to Science Series is designed for grades 5–8+. This series will introduce the following topics: Simple Machines, Electricity and Magnetism, Rocks and Minerals, Atmosphere and Weather, Chemistry, Light and Color, The Solar System, and Sound. Each book will contain an introduction to the topic, naive concepts, inquiry activities, content integration, materials lists, children's literature connections, curriculum resources, assessment documents, and a bibliography. Students will develop an understanding of the concepts and processes of science through the use of good scientific techniques. Students will be engaged in higher-level thinking skills while doing fun and interesting activities. All of the activities will be aligned with the National Science Education Standards and National Council of Teachers of Mathematics Standards.

This series is written for classroom teachers, parents, families, and students. The books in this series can be used as a full unit of study or as individual lessons to supplement existing textbooks or curriculum programs. Activities are designed to be pedagogically sound, hands-on, minds-on science activities that support the National Science Education Standards (NSES). Parents and students can use this series as an enhancement to what is being done in the classroom or as a tutorial at home.

The procedures and content background are clearly explained in the introduction and within the individual activities. Materials used in the activities are commonly found in classrooms and homes. If teachers are giving letter grades for the activities, points may be awarded for each level of mastery indicated on the assessment rubrics. If not, simple check marks at the appropriate levels will give students feedback on how well they are doing.

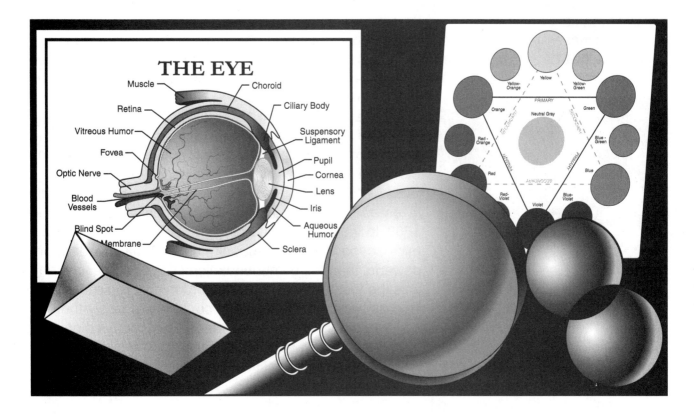

HISTORICAL PERSPECTIVE

The primary source of light on Earth is the sun. Historically, sunlight and shadows were studied and used to tell time. Stonehenge is thought to be an ancient astronomical observatory that dates back to 1848 B.C. The monument at Stonehenge may have served as an accurate astronomical calendar that predicted seasons and eclipses of the sun and moon, calibrated to their rising and setting.

Anaximenes (570–500 B.C.) was one of the first to believe that a rainbow was a natural phenomenon. In 1304, Theodoric of Freibourg, Germany, conducted experiments with globes of water and correctly explained many aspects of the formation of rainbows. René Descartes explained the formation of a rainbow, as well as the formation of clouds, in 1638.

Scientists conducted investigations of the refraction of light. These led to the development of convex lenses as early as 300–291 B.C. Between 1010 and 1029, Alhazen correctly explained how lenses worked and developed parabolic mirrors. Witelo's *Perspectiva*, a treatise on optics dealing with refraction, reflection, and geometrical optics, was published in 1270. Witelo rejected the idea that sight was due to rays emitted from the eyes. People once believed that light traveled from a person's eyes to an object and reflected back to the eye to make sight possible. In 1604, Johannes Kepler described how the eye focused light and showed that light intensity decreased as the square of the distance from the source, a concept known as the *Inverse Square Law*.

The lenses we now use were introduced in the late 1200s. In 1401, Nicholas Krebs used the knowledge of lenses to construct spectacles for the nearsighted, and Leonard Digges invented a surveying telescope in 1551. In 1570, Dutch scientist Hans Lippershey invented the astronomy

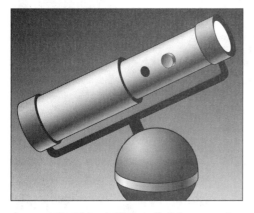

telescope, which Galileo modified to increase the magnification to 30X in 1609. Galileo used it to find the moons of Jupiter, Saturn's rings, the individual stars of the Milky Way, and the phases of Venus. Gregory James was the first to describe a reflecting telescope in 1663.

Zacherias Janssen and Hans Lippershey separately invented the compound microscope between 1590 and 1609. In the mid-1600s, Anton van Leeuwenhoek made a microscope that could magnify up to 270X. It was more powerful than the compound microscopes of the time and was the first to observe and record microscopic life.

In the 1600s, light was described as a form of energy that could travel freely through space. In 1666, Sir Isaac Newton discovered that white light was made up of many colors and that the colors could be separated, using a prism. Leonhard Euler (1746) worked out the mathematics of the refraction of light, by assuming that light is a wave and that different colors corresponded to different wavelengths. From 1160–1169, Robert Grosseteste began to experiment with light, mirrors, and lenses to study rainbows.

HISTORICAL PERSPECTIVE (CONT.)

Newton proposed that light consisted of particles that travel in straight lines through space. At the same time, Christiaan Huygens suggested that light consisted of waves. In 1900, Max Planck proposed that radiant energy comes in little bundles called **quanta**, later called **photons**. His theory helped other scientists to understand that light behaved both as particles and waves, which helped develop the theory of **Quantum Mechanics**.

In 1808, Étienne-Louis Malus discovered that reflected light is polarized, introducing the concept of polarization. Sir David Brewster, in 1812, suggested that there was a relationship between the index of refraction and the angle of incidence, at which reflected light becomes completely polarized.

CONCEPTS

This book will examine light energy. The primary source of light is from the sun. Light energy from the sun warms the earth when it changes to heat energy as it passes through the atmosphere. Light energy is also stored as energy in green plants, which become food for animals and humans or become fossil fuels, such as coal, natural gas, or oil.

Energy from light is **radiant energy**, energy transmitted by electromagnetic waves. Types of radiant energy include infrared rays, radio waves, ultraviolet waves, and X-rays. We only see a tiny part of all different kinds of radiant energy; the part we see is called the **visible spectrum**. Light is visible only when it is the source of light itself, or when it is reflected off something else. Most objects do not emit their own light but reflect it from other sources. Sources of light can be hot, glowing materials, such as the filament or gases in light bulbs. Fire is another source of light, as in burning candles, campfires, etc. The sun and stars are also burning gases that produce light. Sources of light include fluorescent, incandescent, and chemical.

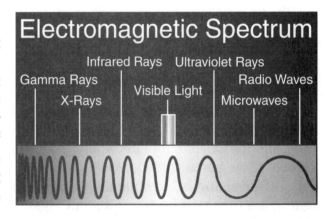

Light travels in straight lines from its source and can change matter. Historically, there have been two theories of how light travels. The **particle theory** suggests that light is made up of particles, and the **wave theory** suggests it is made of waves. Newton proposed that light consisted of particles that travel in straight lines through space. In 1900, Max Planck proposed that radiant energy comes in little bundles called **quanta**, later called **photons**. His theory helped other scientists to understand that light behaved both as particles and waves, which helped develop the theory of **Quantum Mechanics**. In 1905, Einstein's theory of photoelectric effect suggested that light consisted of bundles of concentrated electromagnetic energy that have no mass (photons). Current thought is that light travels in bundles of energy called photons, which are emitted and absorbed as particles, but travel as waves.

In 1880, Albert Michelson conducted an experiment to determine the speed of light. He found that the speed of light in a vacuum was a universal constant. This means that the

3

CONCEPTS (CONT.)

electromagnetic spectrum of light always travels through a vacuum at the constant speed of 186,000 miles per second (300,000 kilometers per second).

Light energy is carried in an electromagnetic wave that is generated by vibrating electrons. The energy from the vibrating electrons is partly electric and partly magnetic; that is why this form of energy is referred to as **electromagnetic waves**. Light waves are classified by frequency into the following types: X-rays, radio waves, microwaves, infrared, visible light, ultraviolet, and gamma rays. The ultraviolet light has a higher frequency than visible light, and infrared has a lower frequency than visible light. Visible light, the light we can see, vibrates at more than 100 trillion times per second, and it includes all of the colors of the spectrum: red, orange, yellow, green, blue, indigo, and violet. (You can use the acronym ROY G. BIV to remember the order of the colors).

The brightness or intensity of light depends on distance and the brightness of the source. Light intensity decreases by the square of the distance. This is known as the *Inverse Square Law* (Intensity is approximately 1 divided by the distance squared, or $\frac{1}{d^2}$).

For example, if the distance from the light source was 2 m, the intensity of the light would be 1/4 of the strength.

Light travels in straight lines. Shadows are formed when objects block out light. This illustrates that light cannot bend around corners without something slowing it down or reflecting it. When a small light source is near an object, or a large source is far away from an object, the image will be sharp. Most shadows are usually blurry, with a dark shadow in the middle and a lighter shadow around the edge. The dark shadow is the **umbra**; the lighter part of the shadow is the **penumbra**. A solar eclipse, when the moon passes between the earth and the sun, is a natural example.

When light strikes an object, it is reflected, absorbed, or passes through. Light colors reflect more light, and dark colors absorb more light. This absorbed light is transformed into heat energy. Objects that allow all light to pass through are called **transparent**. **Translucent** objects allow some light to pass through, and **opaque** objects allow no light to pass through.

Reflection is the bouncing back of a particle or wave off a surface. As light strikes a flat mirror, the light rays bounce off at an equal angle, so the image is clearly shown in the mirror. When light reflects from a mirror, the angle of incidence and the angle of reflection are equal. The **angle of incidence** is the angle formed from the normal light ray that is perpendicular to the surface and the angle made by the incident ray or incoming ray. The **angle of reflection** is the angle made by the normal ray and the outgoing reflected ray. The image you see in a mirror is actually a virtual image because the light does not start at the mirror.

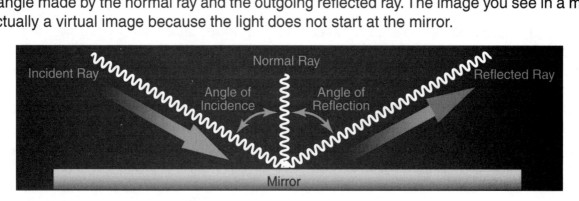

CONCEPTS (CONT.)

Not all mirrors are flat—some are concave mirrors that are curved inward, and some are convex mirrors that are curved outward. When light strikes these mirrors, you will get different images. Looking at your image in the bowl or the back of a shiny spoon will illustrate both of these mirrors. Even though the angle of reflection and angle of incidence are equal, the images formed are different.

Uneven reflection (**diffusion**) happens when the surface is not smooth, which causes the light rays to bounce off at unequal angles. When this happens, there is a reflection, but no clear image.

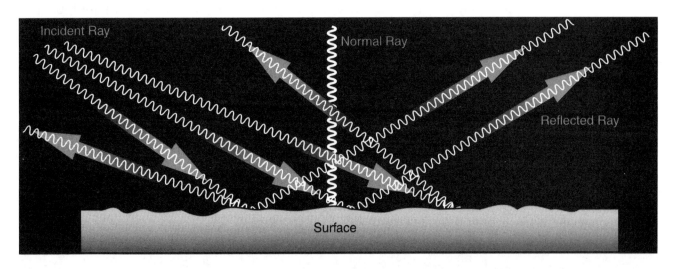

Refraction of light is the bending of light that happens when light travels through different mediums (substances). When light goes from one medium to another and is not at an angle, it does not bend, but the object appears to be closer. If light enters at an angle, it slows down and changes directions, due to the different densities of the mediums. When a straw is put into a glass of water, the straw looks broken, because as the light goes from the air through the glass and the water, which are more dense, it slows down and bends. The **index of refraction** (how much the light bends) is the ratio of the speed of light in a vacuum to the speed of light in a given medium.

CONCEPTS (CONT.)

A **mirage** is caused by atmospheric refraction. On hot days, there may be a layer of hot air on the ground. In hot air, the molecules are farther apart and moving faster than in the cold air above it, and light travels faster through it than the cooler air above it. When the light travels faster through the hot air on the ground than it does in the cooler air above, the light rays are bent. One example of a mirage is when a person is driving on the highway on very hot days, and it sometimes looks as if the pavement is wet.

Lenses work because of refraction. **Lenses** are transparent objects with at least one curved surface. They are carefully shaped to control the bending of light. There are two types of lenses: convex and concave. **Convex lenses** are thicker in the middle and thinner on the edges; light converges or comes together when it passes through the lenses. **Concave lenses** are thin in the middle and thicker on the edges; light diffuses or spreads when it passes through the lenses. In looking at the diagrams below, you will find that only the convex lens can project the flame on the screen, and it is upside-down. The concave lens diffuses or spreads out the light, so it is not projected on the screen. The diagram below has emphasized the light traveling from the candle through the lens to make it easier to understand. As indicated by the diagram, non-polarized light, like the light coming from the candle flame, actually vibrates in all directions. The light coming from the flame is more diffused than the straight lines going to the lens in the diagram.

Light passing through a double concave lens does not project an image on the paper.

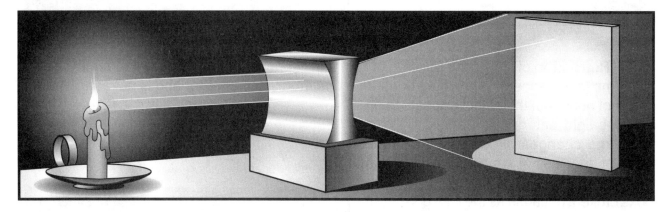

Light passing through a double convex lens projects an upside-down image on the paper.

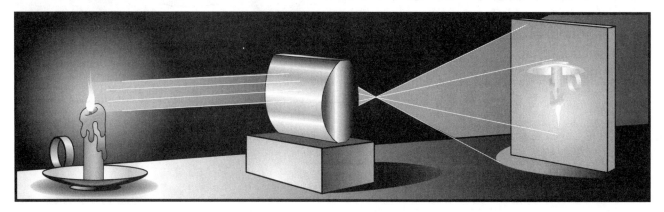

CONCEPTS (CONT.)

Concave lenses correct nearsightedness by making the image smaller but less blurry. Convex lenses correct farsightedness by making the image larger and less blurry; they are also used in refracting telescopes.

White light is made up of many colors. If white light strikes an object, it may absorb or reflect any or all of the parts of the spectrum; that is why we see different colors. We see a red shirt because only red light is reflected off the shirt; all other colors of the spectrum that make up white light are absorbed. White objects reflect all colors; black objects absorb all colors.

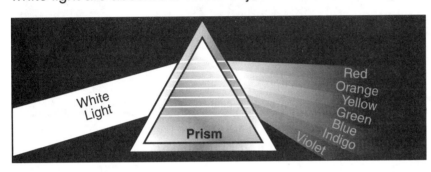

A prism separates light into the colors of the visible spectrum (ROY G. BIV). The separation of light by frequency is called **dispersion**. Different colors of light have different frequencies. As the light enters the prism at an angle and passes through, it slows down and is bent: once going in, and once going out of the prism. Since the speed of light changes, so does the frequency. The lowest frequency is red; the highest is violet.

A prism disperses white light, and a color wheel can put all of the colors of the visible spectrum back together again. A color wheel has pie-shaped sections colored with all of the colors of the visible spectrum, and it is spun around. When the wheel spins around fast enough, individual colors are held by the retina only for a short time so they blend, making the wheel look white.

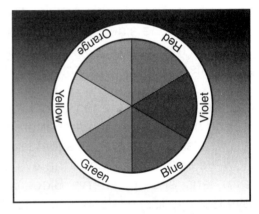

When different colors of light are mixed, they are **additive**. This means that when the colored lights are shone on a white surface, the colors combine to form new colors.

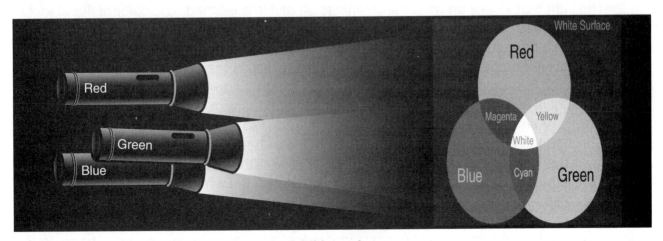

Additive colors

CONCEPTS (CONT.)

When two complementary colors of light are shone on a white surface in the same spot, they are also additive and show as white light. The complementary colors of light are blue and yellow, green and magenta, and red and cyan.

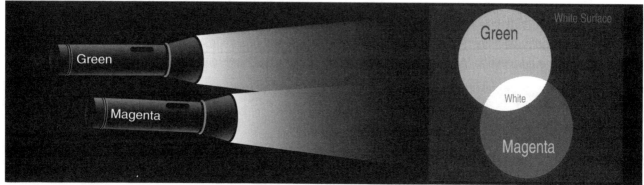

Complementary Colors

Lingering images (persistent vision) can illustrate complementary colors of light. If you stared at a brightly colored piece of paper, and then a piece of white paper, the complementary color will appear on the white paper. This is because the eye becomes tired of staring at the color, so you see the complementary color. Another example of persistent vision is the gerbil in the cage activity. In this activity, the gerbil appears to be inside the cage, even though one image is on one side of the card, and one image is on the other side (see page 65).

In mixing pigments or paints, the colors are **subtractive**, rather than additive. When pigments are mixed, the colors are absorbed instead of reflected. If blue and yellow pigments are mixed together, green is formed. If red is mixed with green, the red absorbs the green, and the green absorbs the red, and the resulting mixture looks black. You will never get white when mixing color pigments. When more than two pigments are mixed, black is made.

Using what we have just learned about the behavior of light and color, we can explain how we see. The inside of the eye consists of the cornea, iris, pupil, sclera (white part of the eye), lens, and optic nerve. Blood vessels in your eye bring food to the eye. The outside of the eye has eyelids, eyelashes, and tear ducts that protect the inside of the eye.

The light that strikes an object and reflects off of it is absorbed. The color of the object is determined by which colors are absorbed or reflected. The light travels to your cornea, a transparent material that acts as a convex lens. The light enters the interior of the eye through the pupil. The pupil is an opening in the center of the iris, which is the colored part of the eye. The iris has muscles that expand and contract the pupil. The pupil opens and closes depending on how much light is available. If there is very little light, it opens wider, and if there is a lot of light, it becomes very small. The light passes through the pupil to another convex lens. As the light passes through the cornea and the lens, it is refracted or bent. These lenses focus the light on the back of the eye, or the retina. Between the lens and the retina is the vitreous humor, a transparent jelly of salts and proteins encased in the sclera, the white part of the eye. The retina is a tissue of light-sensitive cells that absorbs light rays and changes them to electrical signals. Due to the refraction caused by the convex lenses, the image on the retina is upside-down. The retina changes the light rays into electrical signals that are sent through the optic nerve to the brain, where what you are seeing is identified.

NAIVE CONCEPTS

Naive Ideas Related to Light and Color: The naive ideas described below and on page 10 are misconceptions that students may have about light and color.

- Light is associated only with either a source or its effects. Light is not considered to exist independently in space; hence, light is not conceived of as "traveling."
- A shadow is something that exists on its own. Light pushes the shadow away from the object to the wall or the ground, and is thought of as a "dark" reflection of the object.
- Light is not necessarily conserved. It may disappear or be intensified.
- Light from a bulb only extends outward a certain distance, and then stops. How far it extends depends on the brightness of the bulb.
- The effects of light are instantaneous. Light does not travel with a finite speed.
- A mirror reverses everything.
- The mirror image of an object is located on the surface of the mirror. The image is often thought of as a picture on a flat surface.
- Light reflects from a shiny surface in an arbitrary manner.
- Light is reflected from smooth mirror surfaces, but not from non-shiny surfaces.
- Curved mirrors make everything distorted.
- When an object is viewed through a transparent solid or liquid material, the object is seen exactly where it is located.
- When sketching a diagram to show how a lens forms an image of an object, only those light rays that leave the object in straight parallel lines are drawn.
- Blocking part of the lens surface would block the corresponding part of the image.
- An image can be seen on a screen, regardless of where the screen is placed relative to the lens. To see a larger image on a screen, the screen should be moved farther back. An image is always formed at the focal point of the lens.
- The size of the image depends on the size (diameter) of the lens.

NAIVE CONCEPTS (CONT.)

Naive Ideas Related to Color and Vision: The naive ideas described below and on page 9 are misconceptions that students may have about light and color.

- The pupil of the eye is a black object or spot on the surface of the eye.
- The eye receives upright images.
- The lens is the only part of the eye responsible for focusing light.
- The lens forms an image (picture) on the retina. The brain then "looks" at this image, and that is how we see.
- The eye is the only organ for sight; the brain is only for thinking.
- A white light source produces light made up of only one color.
- Sunlight is different from other sources of light, because it contains no color.
- When white light passes through a prism, color is added to the light.
- The primary colors for mixing colored lights are red, blue, and yellow.
- A colored light striking an object produces a shadow behind it that is the same color as the light. For example, when red light strikes an object, a red shadow is formed.
- When white light passes through a colored filter, the filter adds color to the light.
- The mixing of colored paints and pigments follows the same rules as the mixing of colored lights.
- Color is a property of an object and is independent of both the illuminating light and the receiver (eye).
- White light is colorless and clear, enabling you to see the "true" color of an object.
- When a colored light illuminates a colored object, the color of the light mixes with the color of the object.
- Naive explanations of visual phenomena involving color perception usually involve only the properties of the object being observed and do not include the properties of the eye-brain system.

(American Institute of Physics, 2000)

DEFINITION OF TERMS

Bioluminescence: Light given off from certain living things that have the ability to chemically excite the molecules in their bodies

Color: Characteristic of objects that is caused by different qualities of light being reflected or absorbed by them

Diffraction: Bending of a wave around a barrier

Dispersion: Separation of light into colors arranged according to their frequency

Energy: Ability to do work. The scientific definition of work is moving something over a distance.

Infrared Rays: Electromagnetic waves with frequencies lower than the red in the visible light spectrum

Laser: An optical instrument that produces a beam of coherent light, with waves of the same frequency, phase, and direction

Law of Conservation of Energy: Excluding nuclear energy, energy cannot be created or destroyed, only changed.

Lens: A piece of glass or other transparent material that can bend parallel rays of light so that they cross or appear to cross at a single point

Light: A form of radiant energy

Photosynthesis: Process of green plants using sunlight as the energy source to combine carbon dioxide and water to produce sugar and oxygen

Shadow: A shaded area resulting when light is blocked out by an object in its path

Spectrum: The spread of radiation by frequency

Ultraviolet Light: Electromagnetic waves above the frequency of violet light in the visible spectrum

Visible Spectrum: The spread of colors seen when light passes through a prism or diffraction grading

NATIONAL STANDARDS IN SCIENCE AND MATHEMATICS RELATED TO LIGHT AND COLOR

National Science Education Standards (NSES) Content Standards (NRC, 1996)

National Research Council (1996). *National Science Education Standards.* Washington, D.C.: National Academy Press.

Unifying Concepts K–12
Systems, Order, and Organization
Evidence, Models, and Explanation
Change, Constancy, and Measurement
Form and Function

NSES Content Standard A Inquiry
- Abilities necessary to do scientific inquiry
- Understanding about inquiry

NSES Content Standard B 5–8 Transfer Of Energy
- Energy is a property of many substances and is associated with heat, light, electricity, mechanical motion, sound, nuclei, and the nature of a chemical; energy is transferred in many ways.
- Light interacts with matter by transmission, absorption, or scattering. To see an object, light must be emitted by or scattered from it and enter the eye.
- Electrical circuits provide a means of transferring electrical energy when heat, light, sound, and chemical changes are produced.
- In most chemical and nuclear reactions, energy is transferred into or out of the system; heat, light, mechanical motion, or electricity might be involved.
- The sun is the major source of energy for changes on the earth's surface. The sun's energy arrives as light with a range of wavelengths, including visible light, infrared, and ultraviolet radiation. (NRC, 1996)

NSES Content Standard C 5–8 Life Science - Populations and Ecosystems
- The major source of energy in ecosystems is sunlight.

NSES Content Standard D 5–8 Earth and Space - The Earth in the Solar System
- The sun is the major source of energy for phenomena on Earth. This includes plant growth, winds, ocean currents, and the water cycle. Seasons are caused by the variation of the sun's energy hitting the surface, due to the tilt of the earth's rotation on its axis and the length of the day.

NATIONAL STANDARDS IN SCIENCE AND MATHEMATICS RELATED TO LIGHT AND COLOR (CONT.)

National Science Education Standards (NSES) Content Standards (NRC, 1996) (cont.)

NSES Content Standard E 5–8 Science and Technology
- Abilities of Technological Design
- Understanding About Science and Technology

NSES Content Standard F 5–8 Science in Personal and Social Perspectives
- Science and Technology in Society

NSES Content Standard G 5–8 History and Nature of Science
- Science as a Human Endeavor
- Nature of Science
- History of Science

Principles and Standards for School Mathematics (NCTM, 2000)
National Council of Teachers of Mathematics (2000). *Principles and Standards for School Mathematics*. Reston, VA: National Council of Teachers of Mathematics.

Number and Operations
Students will be enabled to ...
- Understand numbers, ways of representing numbers, relationships among numbers, and number systems.
- Understand the meanings of operations and how they relate to one another.
- Compute fluently and make reasonable estimates.

Measurement
Students will be enabled to ...
- Understand measurable attributes of objects and the units, systems, and processes of measurement.
- Apply appropriate techniques, tools, and formulas to determine measurements.

Data Analysis and Probability
Students will be enabled to ...
- Formulate questions that can be addressed with data, and collect, organize, and display relevant data to answer them.
- Select and use appropriate statistical methods to analyze data.
- Develop and evaluate inferences and predictions that are based on data.
- Understand and apply basic concepts of probability.

SCIENCE PROCESS SKILLS

Introduction: Science is organized curiosity, and important parts of this organization are thinking skills or information-processing skills. We ask the question "why?" and then must plan a strategy for answering the question or questions. In the process of answering our questions, we make and carefully record observations, make predictions, identify and control variables, measure, make inferences, and communicate our findings. Additional skills may be called upon, depending upon the nature of our questions. In this way, science is a verb, involving active manipulation of materials and careful thinking. Science is dependent upon language, math, and reading skills, as well as the specialized thinking skills associated with identifying and solving problems.

BASIC PROCESS SKILLS

Classifying: Grouping, ordering, arranging or distributing objects, events, or information into categories based on properties or criteria, according to some method or system.

> **Example –** The skill is being demonstrated if the student is …
> Grouping substances by their physical properties into categories. These categories might include transparent, translucent, and opaque.

Observing: Using the senses (or extensions of the senses) to gather information about an object or event.

> **Example –** The skill is being demonstrated if the student is …
> Seeing and describing the behavior of light.

Measuring: Using both standard and nonstandard measurements or estimates to describe the dimensions of an object or event. Making quantitative observations.

> **Example –** The skill is being demonstrated if the student is …
> Using a ruler to measure the distance between the center of the lens to the focal point or focal length.

Inferring: Making an interpretation or conclusion based on reasoning to explain an observation.

> **Example –** The skill is being demonstrated if the student is …
> Stating that the speed of light changes as it passes through a prism.

Communicating: Communicating ideas through speaking or writing. Students may share the results of investigations, collaborate on solving problems, gather and interpret data both orally and in writing, and use graphs, charts, and diagrams to describe data.

SCIENCE PROCESS SKILLS (CONT.)

> **Example –** The skill is being demonstrated if the student is …
> Describing an event or a set of observations; participating in brainstorming and hypothesizing before an investigation; formulating initial and follow-up questions in the study of a topic; summarizing data, interpreting findings, and offering conclusions; questioning or refuting previous findings; making decisions, or using a graph to show the relationship between distance and the intensity of light.

Predicting: Making a forecast of future events or conditions in the context of previous observations and experiences.

> **Example –** The skill is being demonstrated if the student is …
> Stating where the focal point of various sources of light may be, based on data collected through experimentation and observation.

Manipulating Materials: Handling or treating materials and equipment skillfully and effectively.

> **Example –** The skill is being demonstrated if the student is …
> Arranging equipment and materials needed to conduct an investigation, setting up and conducting an experiment to determine that light travels in a straight line, based on experimentation with shadows.

Replicating: Performing acts that duplicate demonstrated symbols, patterns, or procedures.

> **Example –** The skill is being demonstrated if the student is …
> Constructing an apparatus to determine the focal point of a light source.

Using Numbers: Applying mathematical rules or formulas to calculate quantities or determine relationships from basic measurements.

> **Example –** The skill is being demonstrated if the student is …
> Computing the focal point and focal length.

Developing Vocabulary: Specialized terminology and unique uses of common words in relation to a given topic need to be identified and given meaning.

> **Example –** The skill is being demonstrated if the student is …
> Using context clues, working with definitions, glossaries, dictionaries, word structure (roots, prefixes, suffixes), and synonyms and antonyms to clarify meaning.

SCIENCE PROCESS SKILLS (CONT.)

Questioning: Questions serve to focus inquiry, determine prior knowledge, and establish purposes or expectations for an investigation. An active search for information is promoted when questions are used.

> **Example –** The skill is being demonstrated if the student is ...
> Using what is already known about a topic or concept to formulate questions for further investigation, hypothesizing and predicting prior to gathering data, and formulating questions as new information is acquired.

Using Cues: Key words and symbols convey significant meaning in messages. Organizational patterns facilitate comprehension of major ideas. Graphic features clarify textual information.

> **Example –** The skill is being demonstrated if the student is...
> Listing or underlining words and phrases that carry the most important details, or connecting key words together to express a main idea or concept.

INTEGRATED PROCESS SKILLS

Creating Models: Displaying information by means of graphic illustrations or other multi-sensory representations.

> **Example –** The skill is being demonstrated if the student is ...
> Drawing a graph or diagram, constructing a three-dimensional object, such as a radiometer, constructing a chart or table, or producing a picture or diagram that illustrates information about the behavior of light.

Formulating Hypotheses: Stating or constructing a statement that is testable about what is thought to be the expected outcome of an experiment (based on reasoning).

> **Example –** The skill is being demonstrated if the student is ...
> Making a statement to be used as the basis for an experiment: "If light is a form of energy, it will be able to move an object through a distance."

Generalizing: Drawing general conclusions from particulars.

> **Example –** The skill is being demonstrated if the student is ...
> Making a summary statement following analysis of experimental results: "When light travels through different mediums, other than air, the waves will slow down."

Identifying and Controlling Variables: Recognizing the characteristics of objects or factors in events that are constant or change under different conditions and that can affect an experimental outcome, keeping most variables constant, while manipulating only one variable.

SCIENCE PROCESS SKILLS (CONT.)

> **Example –** The skill is being demonstrated if the student is ...
> Listing or describing the factors that would influence the outcome of an experiment, such as the distance the lens is from the light source and the type of image that would be projected.

Defining Operationally: Stating how to measure a variable in an experiment, defining a variable according to the actions or operations to be performed on or with it.

> **Example –** The skill is being demonstrated if the student is ...
> Defining such things as light, reflection, and refraction in the context of a specific activity.

Recording and Interpreting Data: Collecting bits of information about objects and events that illustrate a specific situation, organizing and analyzing data that have been obtained, and drawing conclusions from it by determining apparent patterns or relationships in the data.

> **Example –** The skill is being demonstrated if the student is ...
> Recording data (taking notes, making lists/outlines, recording numbers on charts/ graphs, making tape recordings, taking photographs, writing numbers of results of observations/measurements) from the investigations to determine if light travels in straight lines.

Making Decisions: Identifying alternatives and choosing a course of action among alternatives after basing the judgment for the selection on justifiable reasons.

> **Example –** The skill is being demonstrated if the student is ...
> Identifying alternative ways to solve a problem through the use of the characteristic behaviors of light; analyzing the consequences of each alternative, such as cost or the effect on other people or the environment; using justifiable reasons as the basis for making choices; choosing freely from the alternatives.

Experimenting: Being able to conduct an experiment, which includes asking an appropriate question, stating a hypothesis, identifying and controlling variables, operationally defining those variables, designing a "fair" experiment, and interpreting the results of an experiment.

> **Example –** The skill is being demonstrated if the student is ...
> Utilizing the entire process of designing, building, and testing various investigations to solve a problem; arranging equipment and materials to conduct an investigation, manipulating the equipment and materials, and conducting the investigation. An experiment was designed and conducted in the "Is Light a Form of Energy?" activity.

Name: _____ Date: _____

STUDENT INQUIRY ACTIVITY **1** : INTRODUCING LIGHT

Topic: Exploring Light

National Standards:
    NSES Unifying Concepts and Processes, (A), (B), (F)
    NCTM Data Analysis and Probability, Measurement

See **National Standards** section for more information on each standard.

Naive Concepts:
- Light is associated only with either a source or its effects. Light is not considered to exist independently in space; hence, light is not conceived of as "traveling."
- A mirror reverses everything.
    (American Institute of Physics, 2000)

Materials:
Flashlight
Mirror
Lens (magnifying glass)
Black and white paper
White button
A variety of objects, different colors and textures
Prism or suncatcher
Shiny, stainless-steel tablespoon
Protractor
Ruler

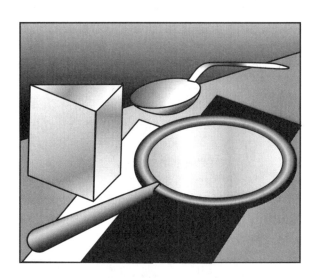

     Science Skills: Students will make **observations** about the properties of light and will **predict** and make **inferences** about the behavior of light. They will be **manipulating** the light source and other objects. In the conclusion section, they will be **communicating** findings. Through this activity, they will be **developing vocabulary** and **identifying** and **controlling variables**, which might affect differences in the behavior of light. They will **record** observations and **interpret** the data collected to determine some of the characteristics of light.

Content Background:
     When light strikes an object, it is reflected, absorbed, or passes through the object. Light colors reflect more light, and dark colors absorb more light. This absorbed light is transformed into heat energy. Objects that allow all light to pass through are called **transparent. Translucent** objects allow some light to pass through, and **opaque** objects allow no light to pass through.
     Reflection is the bouncing back of a particle or wave off a surface. As light strikes a flat mirror, the light rays bounce off at an equal angle, so it shows the image clearly in the mirror. When light reflects from a mirror, the angle of incidence and the angle of reflection are equal. The **angle of incidence** is the angle formed from the normal light ray that is perpendicular to

18

Name: _____ Date: _____

STUDENT INQUIRY ACTIVITY 1: INTRODUCING LIGHT (CONT.)

the surface and the angle made by the incident ray or incoming ray. The **angle of reflection** is the angle made by the normal ray and the outgoing reflected ray. The image you see in a mirror is actually a virtual image, because the light does not start at the mirror.

The **refraction of light** is the bending of light that happens when light travels through different mediums (substances). When light goes from one medium to another and is not at an angle, it does not bend, but the object appears to be closer. If light enters at an angle, it slows down and changes directions due to the different densities of the mediums. When a pencil is put into a glass of water, the pencil looks broken, because as the light goes from the air through the glass and the water, which are more dense, it slows down and bends. The index of refraction, or how much the light bends, is the ratio of the speed of light in a vacuum to the speed of light in a given medium.

Challenge Question: What are some characteristics of light?

Procedure:

1. Explore how light responds when it is shined on the different objects you have collected. Describe some of your observations.

   _____

   _____

   _____

2. Shine the light on each of the colored objects. Describe what happens.

Object	What Happens

Name: _____ Date: _____

STUDENT INQUIRY ACTIVITY 1: INTRODUCING LIGHT (CONT.)

3. Which objects are light sources? How do you know that the objects are light sources?

    _____

    _____

    _____

Exploration/Data Collection:

4. Using the flashlight as a light source, test what happens when the light hits the mirror. Describe what happens.

    _____

    _____

    _____

5. Does the angle at which the light strikes the mirror make a difference as to how the light behaves? Explain.

    _____

    _____

    _____

6. Does the distance from the light source affect what you see? Explain.

    _____

    _____

    _____

7. Using the flashlight as a light source, test what happens when the light passes through the lens. Describe what happens.

    _____

    _____

    _____

Name: _____ Date: _____

STUDENT INQUIRY ACTIVITY **1**: INTRODUCING LIGHT (CONT.)

8. Does the angle at which the light strikes the lens make a difference as to how the light behaves? Explain.

   _____

   _____

   _____

9. Does the distance from the light source affect what you see? Explain.

   _____

   _____

   _____

10. What are some characteristics of light?

   _____

   _____

   _____

Summary:

   Light is reflected or bounces off of flat mirrors. The mirror seems to reverse the image, but it does not. It reflects out what a person standing in front of you sees. It is just the change of viewing perspective that makes it seem reversed. As the distance between the light source and the mirror increases, the brightness decreases. The angle of the mirror changes the direction of the light reflected from the mirror. One characteristic of light is that it can be reflected.

Real-World Application:

   Mirrors are used in everyday life to see how we look, in periscopes, and in cars to see what is behind us. Lenses are used in eyeglasses, microscopes, telescopes, and magnifying glasses.

Integration:

   Mathematics is used in measuring angles and distances, and in collecting, recording, and analyzing data. Language arts skills are used in writing descriptions and conclusions.

Extensions:

   Possible extensions include testing variables, such as brightness or the intensity of light and different light sources.

Name: _____ Date: _____

STUDENT INQUIRY ACTIVITY 1: INTRODUCING LIGHT (CONT.)

Activity Assessment:

Directions: Award points for the level of mastery the student has demonstrated for each skill.

Skill	4 points	3 Points	2 Points	1 Point
Observing	Observes and records observations for all of the objects investigated, including descriptions of light intensity and distance, the angle at which the light reflects, and that light bends or refracts when it passes through a lens or suncatcher. Can identify the flashlight as the light source.	Observes and records observations for some of the objects investigated, including descriptions and the angle at which the light bounces off of the mirror, and that light is distorted when it passes through a lens or suncatcher. Can identify the flashlight as the light source.	Observes and records observations for some of the objects investigated. Can identify the flashlight as the light source.	Observes the mirror, lens, and other objects investigated. Can identify the flashlight as the light source.
Experimenting	Follows directions. Manipulates materials. Performs trial-and-error investigations to find out what happens when the light strikes all of the objects. Records the results of what happens when light strikes each object. Formulates valid conclusions about the effect of the distance and angle of the mirror and what happens when the light passes through the lens.	Follows directions. Manipulates materials. Performs trial-and-error investigations to find out what happens when the light strikes all of the objects. Records the results of what happens when light strikes some of the objects.	Follows directions. Manipulates materials. Performs trial-and-error investigations to find out what happens when the light strikes all of the objects. Records the results of what happens when light strikes the mirror and lens.	Follows directions. Manipulates materials. Performs trial-and-error investigations to find out what happens when the light strikes all of the objects. Records the results of what happens when light strikes one object.
Collecting, recording, and interpreting data	Collects useable data about all objects. Constructs and labels an appropriate data table. Makes valid interpretations of data, including whether light reflects, passes through, is absorbed, or refracts when it strikes the objects.	Collects useable data on some of the objects. Constructs and labels an appropriate data table. Makes valid interpretations of data, including some of the following: whether light reflects, passes through, is absorbed, or refracts when it strikes the objects.	Collects data. Constructs and labels a data table. Makes an attempt to interpret the data.	Collects data. Constructs a data table.

Name: _____ Date: _____

STUDENT INQUIRY ACTIVITY 2: IS LIGHT A FORM OF ENERGY?

Topic: Light Energy

National Standards:
   NSES Unifying Concepts and Processes, (A), (B), (E), (F), (G)
   NCTM Data Analysis and Probability, Measurement

See **National Standards** section for more information on each standard.

Naive Concepts:
- Light is associated only with either a source or its effects. Light is not considered to exist independently in space; hence, light is not conceived of as "traveling."
- Light is not necessarily conserved. It may disappear or be intensified.
  (American Institute of Physics, 2000)
- Reflection and absorption of light cause a radiometer to move.

Materials:
Magnifying glass
Paper
Bright sunlight
Metal tray or nonflammable surface
Ruler

   Science Skills: Students will make **observations** about the properties of light, and will **predict** and make **inferences** as to whether or not light is a form of energy. They will be **classifying** whether or not light is energy and **manipulating** materials, such as the magnifying glass and ruler. In the conclusion section, students will be **communicating** findings and **developing vocabulary**. They will be **collecting**, **recording**, **analyzing**, and **interpreting** the data collected to determine whether or not light is a form of energy.

Content Background:
   Energy from light is radiant energy. The Law of Conservation of Energy states that energy cannot be created or destroyed, but it can be changed from one form to another. Kinds of radiant energy include infrared rays, radio waves, ultraviolet waves, and X-rays. We only see a tiny part of all different kinds of radiant energy; the part we see is called the **visible spectrum**. Light is visible only when it is the source of light or when it is reflected off something else. Most objects do not emit their own light but reflect it from other sources. Sources of light can be hot, glowing materials, such as the filament or gases in light bulbs. Fire is another source of light, as in burning candles, campfires, etc. The sun and stars are also burning gases that produce light. Sources of light include fluorescent, incandescent, and chemical.
   Light energy is carried in an electromagnetic wave that is generated by vibrating electrons. The energy from the vibrating electrons is partly electric and partly magnetic, and is called **electromagnetic waves**. Light is only a small portion of a broader family of electromagnetic

Name: _____   Date: _____

STUDENT INQUIRY ACTIVITY 2 : IS LIGHT A FORM OF ENERGY? (CONT.)

waves called the **electromagnetic spectrum**. Light waves are classified by frequency. When light strikes an object, it is reflected, absorbed, or passes through the object. Objects that allow all light to pass through are called **transparent**. **Translucent** objects allow some light to pass through, and **opaque** objects allow no light to pass through. Light colors reflect more light, and dark colors absorb more light. Absorbed light is transformed into heat energy.

Investigation:

Is light a form of energy?

Energy is the ability to do work. The scientific definition of **work** is moving something over a distance. Knowing these definitions, state a hypothesis to test whether or not light is a form of energy.

Hypothesis: A hypothesis is a statement of a proposed explanation of the results.

State your hypothesis. _____

_____

Light is a form of energy if _____

_____

Challenge Question: Is light a form of energy?

Procedure:

1. Find a place where the sun shines directly into the room, or do the activity outside.

2. Lay the paper on the tray.

3. Hold the magnifying glass between the sun and the paper.

Name: _____ Date: _____

STUDENT INQUIRY ACTIVITY 2: IS LIGHT A FORM OF ENERGY? (CONT.)

4. What do you see on the paper?

   _____

   _____

   _____

5. Move the magnifying glass up and down. What happens to the light on the paper?

   _____

   _____

   _____

Exploration/Data Collection:

Using the materials listed, conduct the following investigation to determine if light is a form of energy.

6. What happens when a magnifying glass is placed between the sun and a piece of paper?

   _____

   _____

   _____

7. From the experiment above, how can you focus the sunlight so that it shows a small point of light on the paper?

   _____

   _____

   _____

Name: _____ Date: _____

STUDENT INQUIRY ACTIVITY 2: IS LIGHT A FORM OF ENERGY? (CONT.)

8. The point of light on the paper is the focal point of the lens. Measure the distance between the center of the magnifying glass and the focal point on the paper. This is your focal length. Hold the magnifying glass in this position and observe what happens. Record what happens as the sun passes through the magnifying glass onto the paper.

_____

_____

_____

_____

9. Explain what happened.

_____

_____

_____

_____

10. Light energy has been transformed into heat energy. What happens to the molecules of a substance when they are heated?

_____

_____

_____

_____

11. Is light a form of energy? How do you know?

_____

_____

_____

_____

Name: _____ Date: _____

STUDENT INQUIRY ACTIVITY 2: IS LIGHT A FORM OF ENERGY? (CONT.)

Summary:

Light energy from the sun converges into one point as it passes through the double convex lens of the magnifying glass. When the magnifying glass is moved up and down, you can find the focal point of the lens. The distance between the center of the lens and the focal point on the paper is the focal length of the lens. When the light strikes the paper, the molecules of the paper begin moving faster and faster, and eventually burn. In this case, the light energy has been converted to heat energy.

Real-World Application:

Radiometers used in the study of space are based on the same principle. The radiometer uses heat energy from the light to make it spin. Light energy (photons) can also be used to push solar sails through space. Unlike the radiometer, the photons bounce off of the reflective material on the sails, resulting in a push. The greater the area of the sail, the greater the push. Cosmos I is an example of a solar sail.

Colored construction paper, cloth, and wallpaper fade, due to sunlight shining through the window glass.

Extensions:

Build Your Own Cosmos I Solar Sail
    http://www.themosh.org/psd2002/athome/lesson one.asp

Animation of Cosmos I Solar Sail
    http://www.planetary.org/solarsail/images/opening mov02.swf

Cosmos I Updated Information
    http://www.planetary.org/solarsail/index2.html

Investigating Different Forms of Energy
    http://www.msnucleus.org/membership/html/k-6/as/physics/2/asp2.html

Name: _____   Date: _____

STUDENT INQUIRY ACTIVITY 2: IS LIGHT A FORM OF ENERGY? (CONT.)

Activity Assessment:

Directions: Mark the statement that best describes the student's level of mastery.

_____   Made a hypothesis and conducted an investigation to test the hypothesis, using the materials given, to determine if light is a form of energy. Student demonstrated the ability to collect, record, and analyze data to draw the conclusion that light is a form of energy, because it can move the molecules of the paper so fast that the paper burns.

_____   Made a hypothesis and conducted an investigation to test the hypothesis, using the materials given, to determine if light is a form of energy. Student demonstrated the ability to collect, record, and analyze data to draw the conclusions.

_____   Made a hypothesis and conducted an investigation to test the hypothesis using the materials given, to determine if light is a form of energy. Student demonstrated the ability to collect, record, and analyze data.

Name: _____ Date: _____

STUDENT INQUIRY ACTIVITY 3: HOW DOES LIGHT TRAVEL?

Topic: Shadows

National Standards:
NSES Unifying Concepts and Processes, (A), (B)
NCTM Data Collection and Analysis

See **National Standards** section for more information on each standard.

Naive Concepts:
• A shadow is something that exists on its own. Light pushes the shadow away from the object to the wall or the ground, and is thought of as a "dark" reflection of the object.
(American Institute of Physics, 2000)

Materials:
6 different solid objects
Flashlight
White paper

Science Skills: Students will make **observations** about the properties of light, and will **predict** and **make inferences** as to what causes shadows. They will be **manipulating** materials, such as the light source and different objects. In the conclusion section, they will be **communicating** findings and **developing vocabulary**. Students will be required to **identify** and **control variables**, which might affect differences in the way light behaves. They will be **collecting**, **recording**, **analyzing**, and **interpreting** data, and **inferring** and **using cues** to determine what causes shadows.

Content Background:
Light travels in straight lines from its source, and can change matter. Historically, there have been two theories as to how light travels. The **particle theory** suggests that light is made of particles, and the **wave theory** suggests that it is made of waves. Newton proposed that light consists of particles that travel in straight lines through space. In 1900, Max Planck proposed that radiant energy comes in little bundles called **quanta**, later called **photons**. His theory helped other scientists understand that light behaves both as particles and waves, and helped to develop the theory of **Quantum Mechanics**. In 1905, Einstein's theory of photoelectric effect suggested that light consisted of bundles of concentrated electromagnetic energy that have no mass (photons). Current thought is that light travels in bundles of energy called photons that are emitted and absorbed as particles, but they travel as waves.

Shadows are formed when objects block out light. This illustrates that light cannot bend around corners without something slowing it down or reflecting it. When a small light source is near an object or a large source is far away from an object, the image will be sharp. Most shadows are usually blurry, with a dark shadow in the middle and a lighter shadow around the edge. The dark shadow is the **umbra**, and the lighter part of the shadow is the **penumbra**. A solar eclipse, when the moon passes between the earth and the sun, is a natural example.

29

Name: _____ Date: _____

STUDENT INQUIRY ACTIVITY 3: HOW DOES LIGHT TRAVEL? (CONT.)

When light strikes an object, it is reflected, absorbed, or passes through the object. Light colors reflect more light, and dark colors absorb more light. This absorbed light is transformed into heat energy. Objects that allow all light to pass through are called **transparent**. **Translucent** objects allow some light to pass through, and **opaque** objects allow no light to pass through.

Challenge Question: How are shadows formed?

Procedure:

1. Shine the light on the white paper.

2. Put one of the objects between the light and the white paper.

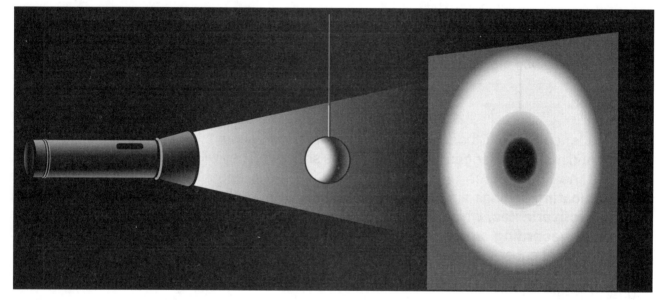

3. Describe what happens. Explain why this happens.

_____

_____

_____

_____

4. Predict what will happen when you try the other objects.

_____

_____

_____

_____

Name: _____ Date: _____

STUDENT INQUIRY ACTIVITY 3: HOW DOES LIGHT TRAVEL? (CONT.)

Exploration/Data Collection:

5. Test the other objects by putting them between the white paper and light source.

6. Observe the images formed.

7. Draw pictures of the object and the shadow.

Object	A picture of the object	A picture of the shadow formed

8. What do you notice about the object and the shadow formed for each object?

_____

_____

_____

9. Does the angle at which the light hits the object change the shadow?

_____

_____

_____

Name: _____ Date: _____

STUDENT INQUIRY ACTIVITY 3 : HOW DOES LIGHT TRAVEL? (CONT.)

10. How could you find out if the angle made a difference?

_____

_____

_____

11. Try what you suggested in #10. Did it change the shadow? Explain.

_____

_____

_____

12. Does the distance that the light is from the object affect the shadow formed?

_____

_____

_____

13. How could you find out if the distance made the shadow look different?

_____

_____

_____

14. Try what you suggested in #13. Did it change the shadow?

_____

_____

_____

15. Based on the data gathered from this investigation, what is a characteristic of light?

_____

_____

_____

_____

Name: _____ Date: _____

STUDENT INQUIRY ACTIVITY 3: HOW DOES LIGHT TRAVEL? (CONT.)

Summary:

Light travels in straight lines. This is demonstrated by the formation of shadows. If the shadows did not form, it would show that light can bend around objects in its path. Shadows are formed by objects blocking out light, illustrating that light cannot bend around corners without something slowing it down or reflecting it. When a small light source is near an object or a large source far from an object, the image will be sharp. Most shadows are usually blurry, but will look similar to the outline of the object. The shadow does change when the light is moved closer or farther away from the object. The angle at which the light hits the object will also change the shadow's shape.

Real-World Application:

Shadows have been used over the ages to track the passage of time, i.e., sundials.

Integration:

History and language arts can be integrated by researching and reporting information on sundials, Stonehenge, and historical timepieces and calendars.

Literature connections:

Shel Silverstein (1981) *Shadow Race;*

Robert Louis Stevenson's "My Shadow," found in his book *A Child's Garden of Verses;*

The Story of Clocks and Calendars: Marking a Millennium by Betsy Maestro.

Extensions:

Trees or other objects can be used as sundials to measure time. A shadow can also be used to measure the height of a tree.

Name: _____   Date: _____

STUDENT INQUIRY ACTIVITY 3: HOW DOES LIGHT TRAVEL? (CONT.)

Activity Assessment:

Directions: Mark the level of mastery the student demonstates.

_____ Students are able to explain all of the following:
- Light travels in straight lines.
- Shadows are formed when objects block out light.
- When a small light source is near an object, the object will be sharp.
- When a large light source is far from an object, the image will be sharp.
- Most shadows are usually blurry, but will look similar to the outline of the object.
- The shadow does change when the light is moved closer or farther away from the object.
- The angle at which the light hits the object will also change the shadow's shape.
- Shadows show that light travels in straight lines.

_____ Students are able to explain four of the following:
- Light travels in straight lines.
- Shadows are formed when objects block out light.
- When a small light source is near an object, the object will be sharp.
- When a large light source is far from an object, the image will be sharp.
- Most shadows are usually blurry, but will look similar to the outline of the object.
- The shadow does change when the light is moved closer or farther away from the object.
- The angle at which the light hits the object will also change the shadow's shape.
- Shadows show that light travels in straight lines.

_____ Students are able to explain that:
- Shadows are formed when objects block out light.
- The image changes when the distance between the light and the object increases or decreases.
- The angle at which the light hits the object will also change the shadow's shape.
- Shadows show that light travels in straight lines.

Name: _____ Date: _____

STUDENT INQUIRY ACTIVITY 4: HOW DOES LIGHT BEHAVE WHEN IT STRIKES A MIRROR?

Topic: Reflection

National Standards:
 NSES Unifying Concepts (A), (B), (E)
 NCTM Number and Operations, Measurement, Data Analysis and Probability

See **National Standards** sections for more information about each standard.

Naive Concepts:
* A mirror reverses everything.
* The mirror image of an object is located on the surface of the mirror. The image is often thought of as a picture on a flat surface.
* Light reflects from a shiny surface in an arbitrary manner.
* Light is reflected from smooth mirror surfaces, but not from non-shiny surfaces.
* Curved mirrors make everything distorted.
  (American Institute of Physics, 2000)

Materials:
Flat mirror
Large, shiny metal spoon
Flashlight
Protractor
White paper and pencil
Ruler

 Science Skills: Students will be **observing**, making **predictions**, and **formulating a hypothesis** and **questions** by **manipulating** materials to conduct an **experiment**, **using numbers** to measure angles and distance, and **calculating** the angle of incidence and reflection. Students will be **collecting**, **recording**, and **interpreting** data and **developing** the **vocabulary** to **communicate** the results of their findings.

Content Background:
 When light strikes an object, it is reflected, absorbed, or passes through the object. Objects that allow all light to pass through are called **transparent**. **Translucent** objects allow some light to pass through, and **opaque** objects allow no light to pass through. Light colors reflect more light, and dark colors absorb more light. Absorbed light is transformed into heat energy.
 Reflection is the bouncing back of a particle or wave off a surface. Instead of going *through* the material, it bounces off. An example of this is light hitting a plane surface or flat mirror. The smooth surface of the flat mirror allows all of the light rays to bounce off at an equal

Name: _____   Date: _____

STUDENT INQUIRY ACTIVITY 4 : HOW DOES LIGHT BEHAVE WHEN IT STRIKES A MIRROR? (CONT.)

angle, so the image is clearly shown in the mirror. Uneven reflection **(diffusion)** occurs when the surface is not as smooth, and the light rays bounce off at unequal angles. When this happens, there is a reflection, but no clear image.

The angle of incidence and the angle of reflection are equal. The **angle of incidence** is the angle formed from the normal light ray that is perpendicular to the surface and the angle made by the incident ray or incoming ray. The **angle of reflection** is the angle made by the normal ray and the outgoing reflected ray. The image you see in a mirror is actually a virtual image, because the light does not start at the mirror.

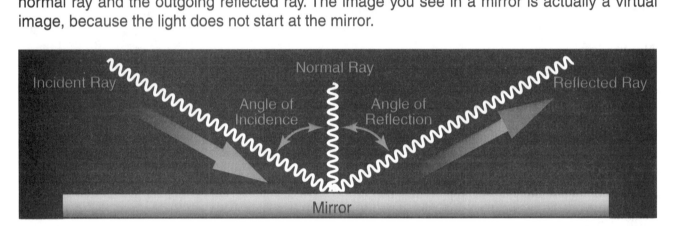

All mirrors are not flat; some are concave mirrors that are curved inward, and some are convex mirrors that are curved outward. When light strikes each of these mirrors, you will get different images. When you look at your image in the bowl or the back of a shiny spoon, this illustrates both types of mirrors. Even though the angle of reflection and angle of incidence are equal, the images formed are different.

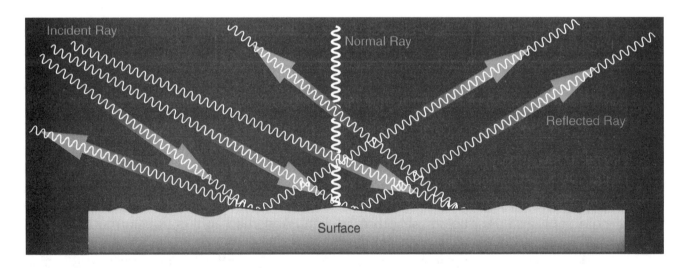

Name: _____ Date: _____

STUDENT INQUIRY ACTIVITY 4 : HOW DOES LIGHT BEHAVE WHEN IT STRIKES A MIRROR? (CONT.)

Challenge Question: How does light behave when it strikes a mirror?

Procedure:

1. Draw a line straight across the bottom of the white sheet of paper.

2. Draw a second line in the middle of the paper, perpendicular to the line at the bottom of the sheet.

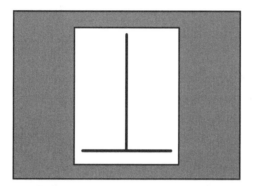

3. Place the mirror on the horizontal line.

4. Place a flashlight on the line perpendicular to the mirror, and shine the light on the mirror.

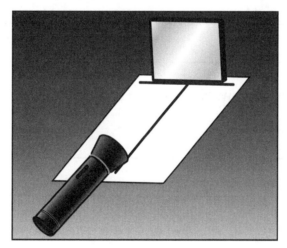

5. Describe what you see.

_____

_____

_____

Name: _____ Date: _____

STUDENT INQUIRY ACTIVITY 4: HOW DOES LIGHT BEHAVE WHEN IT STRIKES A MIRROR? (CONT.)

6. Put your face in line with the perpendicular line. Describe what you see.

   _____

   _____

   _____

Data Collection and Analysis:
Investigation #1

7. Look at yourself in the mirror. Describe the image you see.

   _____

   _____

8. How is the image in #7 different from the image in #6? Why?

   _____

   _____

   _____

9. Look at your image in the bowl of the spoon and on the back of the spoon. Describe what you see.

   _____

   _____

10. How is the image different in the bowl or on the back of the spoon? Why?

   _____

   _____

   _____

Name: _____ Date: _____

STUDENT INQUIRY ACTIVITY 4: HOW DOES LIGHT BEHAVE WHEN IT STRIKES A MIRROR? (CONT.)

11. Draw what you see.

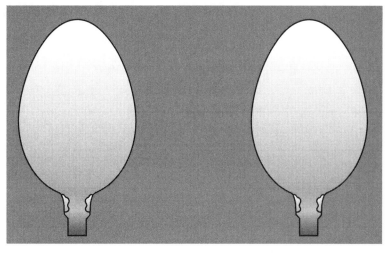

Spoon Bowl   **Spoon Back**

12. Explain how the distance at which you have the spoon from your face affects what the image looks like.

_____

_____

13. How does the way you hold the spoon affect the image you see?

_____

_____

14. Draw what you see.

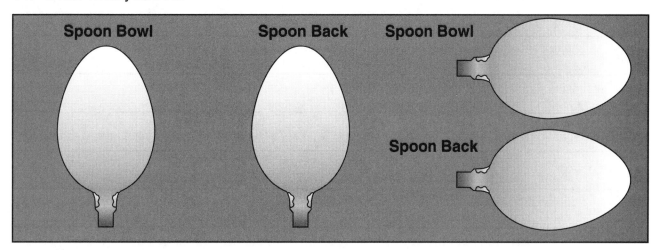

Spoon Bowl   **Spoon Back**   **Spoon Bowl**

Spoon Back

Name: _____ Date: _____

Student Inquiry Activity 4: How Does Light Behave When It Strikes a Mirror? (cont.)

15. Using the paper you prepared with the perpendicular lines, shine the light straight onto the mirror.

16. Predict what you think will happen as the angle of the mirror changes.

_____

_____

_____

17. Design an investigation, using the mirror, to find out how the angle of the mirror affects what happens when the light hits it.

18. List the materials needed.

_____

_____

_____

_____

19. Describe what will be done during the investigation.

_____

_____

_____

_____

_____

_____

Light and Color

Student Inquiry Activity 4: How Does Light Behave When It Strikes a Mirror?

Name: _____ Date: _____

STUDENT INQUIRY ACTIVITY 4: HOW DOES LIGHT BEHAVE WHEN IT STRIKES A MIRROR? (CONT.)

20. Identify what variables could affect what happens during the investigation, and describe how you will control some of them.

_____

_____

_____

21. Using the investigation you designed, collect information and record it in a data table similar to the one below.

Investigation #1
"How does the angle of the mirror affect what happens when the light hits the mirror?"

Variable Tested	Light Source	Results
Angle of mirror in degrees	Distance between light and mirror (cm)	
180 degrees		
135 degrees		
45 degrees		
20 degrees		

22. Looking at the data collected, how does the angle of the mirror affect what happens when the light hits the mirror?

_____

_____

_____

_____

Name: _____ Date: _____

STUDENT INQUIRY ACTIVITY 4: HOW DOES LIGHT BEHAVE WHEN IT STRIKES A MIRROR? (CONT.)

Investigation #2

Materials:
Kaleidoscope made from:
   3 mirrors
   Duct tape
   Large paper clip
   Large cat's-eye marble

23. Construct a kaleidoscope.
24. Place the mirrors in the form of a triangle, with the shiny side inside.
25. Duct-tape the mirrors together. Completely cover the outside of the mirrors with tape. This will keep the mirrors from shattering if they are dropped.
26. Make a holder for the marble out of the paper clip and duct-tape it to one end of the kaleidoscope.

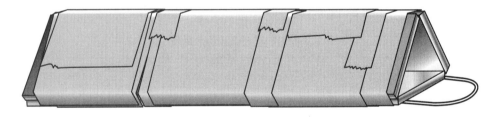

27. Put the marble on the paper clip.

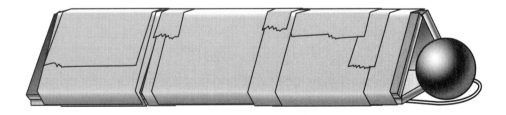

28. Look through the other end, and describe what you see.

_____

_____

_____

_____

Name: _____ Date: _____

Student Inquiry Activity 4 : How Does Light Behave When It Strikes a Mirror? (cont.)

29. Based on Investigation #2, describe the causes of the image you are seeing.

_____

_____

_____

_____

_____

Summary:

Light strikes an object and reflects off it to the mirror and then reflects or bounces off the mirrored surfaces. The shape of the mirror and the angle at which the light hits the mirror will affect the image that is seen. The bowl of the spoon acts as a concave mirror, and the back of the spoon acts as a convex mirror. In the concave mirror, the image is larger than in the convex, farther from the actual image, and inverted or turned upside-down. In the convex mirror, the image is right-side-up, but it is smaller. If the spoon is moved farther away, the image of your whole body is in the spoon. If you look at the image with the spoon handle down, the image is long and thin, and if it is to one side or the other, the image is short and wide. The brightness or intensity of the light increases when the light source is closer to the mirror and decreases as the light is farther away.

Real-World Application:

Mirrors are used in reflecting telescopes, microscopes, solar reflectors on satellites, and fun houses.

Integration:

Measuring the distance and angles and collecting, recording, and analyzing data are also skills used in mathematics. Language arts in this activity include writing and communication of observations and results.

Extensions:

Identifying other objects that act as mirrors and where mirrors are used in our everyday lives.

Name: _____ Date: _____

STUDENT INQUIRY ACTIVITY 4: HOW DOES LIGHT BEHAVE WHEN IT STRIKES A MIRROR? (CONT.)

Activity Assessment:

Directions: Award points based on the level of mastery of the student.

4 points
Student included all nine of the following:
- Light reflects or bounces off of the mirrored surfaces.
- The shape of the mirror changes the image seen.
- The angle at which the light hits the mirror will affect the image that is seen.
- In a concave mirror (the bowl of the spoon), the image is larger than in the convex, farther from the actual image, and inverted or turned upside-down.
- In the convex mirror (the back of the spoon), the image is right-side-up and smaller.
- The farther away the spoon is, the more of the image can be seen.
- With the spoon handle down, the image is long and thin.
- With the spoon handle to one side or the other, the image is short and wide.
- The brightness or intensity of the light increases when the light source is close to the mirror and decreases as the light is moved farther away.

3 points
Student included at least five of the following:
- Light reflects or bounces off of the mirrored surfaces.
- The shape of the mirror changes the image seen.
- The angle at which the light hits the mirror will affect the image that is seen.
- In a concave mirror (the bowl of the spoon), the image is larger than in the convex, farther from the actual image, and inverted or turned upside-down.
- In the convex mirror (the back of the spoon), the image is right-side-up and smaller.
- The farther away the spoon is, the more of the image can be seen.
- With the spoon handle down, the image is long and thin.
- With the spoon handle to one side or the other, the image is short and wide.
- The brightness or intensity of the light increases when the light source is close to the mirror and decreases as the light is moved farther away.

2 points
Student included all four of the following:
- Light reflects or bounces off of the mirrored surfaces.
- The shape of the mirror changes the image seen.
- The distance between the actual object and the mirror affects the image you see in the mirror.
- The direction of the spoon affects the image.

1 point
Student included both of the following:
- The shape of the mirror changes the image seen.
- The distance between the actual object and the mirror affects the image you see in the mirror.

Name: _____ Date: _____

STUDENT INQUIRY ACTIVITY 5 : WHAT HAPPENS WHEN LIGHT PASSES THROUGH A DOUBLE CONVEX LENS?

Topic: Refraction

National Standards:
   NSES Unifying Concepts, (A), (B)
   NCTM Number and Operations, Measurement, Data Analysis and Probability

See **National Standards** section for more information on each standard.

Naive Concepts:
- When an object is viewed through a transparent solid or liquid material, the object is seen exactly where it is located.
- When sketching a diagram to show how a lens forms an image of an object, only those light rays that leave the object in straight parallel lines are drawn.
- Blocking part of the lens surface would block the corresponding part of the image.
- The purpose of a surface is to capture the image so that it can be seen. The surface is necessary for the image to be formed. Without a surface, there is no image.
- An image can be seen on a surface regardless of where the surface is placed relative to the lens. In actuality, to see a larger image on the surface, it should be moved farther back, and an image is always formed at the focal point of the lens.
- The size of the image depends on the size (diameter) of the lens.
- When a wave moves through a medium, particles of the medium move along with the wave. (American Institute of Physics, 2000)

Materials:
Double convex lens (magnifying glass)
Light source
White paper
Meter stick
Clay
Match

WARNING: This activity involves an open flame. This should be done with adult supervision and away from flammable materials. **(Goggles are recommended.)**

   Science Skills: Students will be **observing**, making **predictions**, and **formulating** a **hypothesis** and **questions** about light by **manipulating** materials to **conduct an experiment**, using numbers to **measure** the focal length of the lens. Students will be **collecting**, **recording**, and **interpreting** data, and **developing vocabulary** to communicate the results of their findings. Based on their findings, students will be able to **infer** what happens when light travels through a medium other than air.

Name: _____ Date: _____

STUDENT INQUIRY ACTIVITY 5: WHAT HAPPENS WHEN LIGHT PASSES THROUGH A DOUBLE CONVEX LENS? (CONT.)

Content Background:

The **refraction of light** is the bending of light that happens when light travels through different mediums (substances). When light goes from one medium to another, not at an angle, it does not bend, but the object appears to be closer. If light enters at an angle, it slows down and changes directions, due to the different densities of the mediums. When a pencil is put into a glass of water, the pencil looks broken, because as the light goes from the air through the glass and the water, which are more dense, it slows down and bends. The **index of refraction** (how much the light bends) is the ratio of the speed of light in a vacuum to the speed of light in a given medium.

A **mirage** is caused by atmospheric refraction. On hot days, there may be a layer of hot air on the ground. In hot air, the molecules are farther apart and moving faster than in the cold air above it, and light travels faster through the hot layer than through the cooler air. When this happens, the light rays bend. An example of a mirage is when you are driving on the highway on very hot days, and the pavement sometimes looks as if it is wet.

Lenses work because of refraction. Lenses are transparent objects with at least one curved surface. They are carefully shaped to control the bending of light. There are two types of lenses: convex and concave. **Convex lenses** are thicker in the middle and thinner on the edges, and light converges or comes together when it passes through the lens. **Concave lenses** are thin in the middle and thicker on the edges, and light diffuses, or spreads, when it passes through the lens. In looking at the diagrams below, you will find that only the convex lens can project the flame on the screen, and it is upside-down. The concave lens diffuses or spreads out the light, so it is not projected on the screen. The diagram below has emphasized the light traveling from the candle through the lens to make it easier to understand. As indicated by the diagram, non-polarized light, like the light coming from the candle flame, actually vibrates in all directions. The light coming from the flame is actually more diffused than the straight lines going to the lens in the diagram.

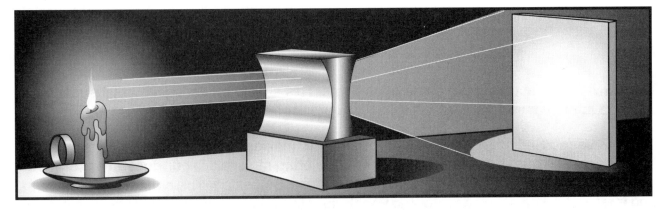

Double Concave Lens

46

Name: _____ Date: _____

STUDENT INQUIRY ACTIVITY 5: WHAT HAPPENS WHEN LIGHT PASSES THROUGH A DOUBLE CONVEX LENS? (CONT.)

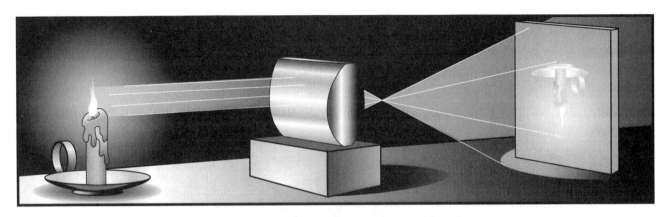

Double Convex Lens

Concave lenses correct nearsightedness by making the image smaller but less blurry. Convex lenses correct farsightedness by making the image larger and less blurry. Convex lenses are also used in refracting telescopes.

Challenge Question: How does light behave when it passes through a double convex lens?

Procedure:

1. Fill a clear glass half-full of water.

2. Place a pencil in the glass.

3. Look through the side of the glass and describe what you see.

   _____

   _____

   _____

4. Explain the results from #3.

   _____

   _____

   _____

   _____

Name: _____ Date: _____

STUDENT INQUIRY ACTIVITY 5: WHAT HAPPENS WHEN LIGHT PASSES THROUGH A DOUBLE CONVEX LENS? (CONT.)

Exploration/Data Collection:

WARNING: This activity involves an open flame. This should be done with adult supervision and away from flammable materials. **(Goggles are recommended.)**

5. Using the setup below, design an investigation using the lens to find out what happens when the light passes through the lens.

6. Describe what will be done during the investigation.

_____

_____

_____

_____

_____

_____

_____

Name: _____ Date: _____

STUDENT INQUIRY ACTIVITY 5: WHAT HAPPENS WHEN LIGHT PASSES THROUGH A DOUBLE CONVEX LENS? (CONT.)

7. Identify what variables could affect the results of the investigation (i.e., the distance between the light source and lens, or whether the light passes straight through the face of the lens or through the side of the lens).

    _____

    _____

    _____

8. Describe how you will control some of the variables you identified.

    _____

    _____

    _____

9. On your own paper, create a data table like the one below to record your data.

Variable tested	Variables Controlled	Results

10. Using the data collected, what happens when the light passes through the lens?

    _____

    _____

    _____

11. Explain the results from #10.

    _____

    _____

    _____

Name: _____ Date: _____

STUDENT INQUIRY ACTIVITY 5: WHAT HAPPENS WHEN LIGHT PASSES THROUGH A DOUBLE CONVEX LENS? (CONT.)

Summary:

The **refraction of light** is the bending of light. This happens when light travels through substances with different densities. When light goes from one medium to another, and not at an angle, it does not bend, but the object appears to be closer. If light enters a transparent material at an angle, it slows down and changes directions. The speed of light changes as it passes into a different medium or substance with a different density. The speed also changes as it passes through substances of various temperatures. This is due to the change in density caused by adding or taking away heat. When most materials are heated, the molecules spread farther apart, making it less dense; when they are cooled, the molecules come closer together, increasing the density.

When a pencil is put into a glass of water, the pencil looks broken, because as the light moves from the air through the glass and the water, it slows down and bends. The water and glass are denser than the air, so the light slows down and bends; it makes the pencil look bent or broken.

When the light of the candle passes through the double convex lens, the light slows down and bends, forming an inverted image on the white paper.

Real-World Application:

Concave lenses correct nearsightedness by making the image smaller but less blurry. When you look at the edge of a lens in eyeglasses that correct nearsightedness, the concave lens is thicker on the edges than in the middle. Convex lenses correct farsightedness by making the image larger and less blurry. When you examine the edge of a lens in eyeglasses that correct farsightedness, the convex lens is thicker in the middle and thinner on the edges.

Integration:

Mathematics is integrated with the data collection, recording, analysis, and measurement of the distance between the lens and the object and the lens and the white paper.

Convex Eyeglasses   Concave Eyeglasses

STUDENT INQUIRY ACTIVITY 5: WHAT HAPPENS WHEN LIGHT PASSES THROUGH A DOUBLE CONVEX LENS? (CONT.)

Extensions:

Extensions for this activity could include the following:

- Investigating the effect of moving the lens toward and away from the candle and changing the distances between the lens and the screen.
- Conducting an investigation to find out how light is affected using a double concave lens and comparing the results.
- Testing larger and smaller lenses or thicker and thinner lenses.
- Constructing a pinhole camera from two paper cups, a pin, translucent paper (i.e., wax paper or tissue paper), and clear tape. See diagram below.

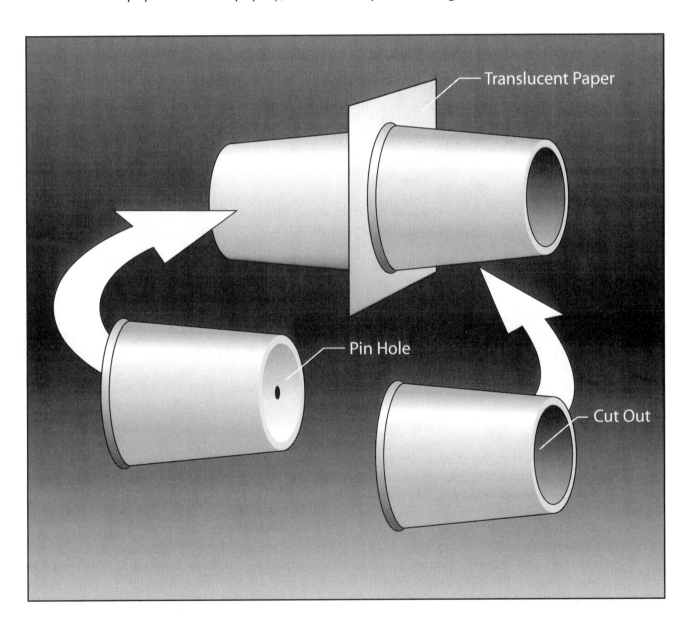

Name: _____ Date: _____

STUDENT INQUIRY ACTIVITY **5**: WHAT HAPPENS WHEN LIGHT PASSES THROUGH A DOUBLE CONVEX LENS? (CONT.)

Activity Assessment:

Directions: Award points based on the level of mastery of the student.

3 points

Processes

Student was able to:
- Design an investigation to show what happens when light goes through the lens.
- Select and use processes of science appropriately, including detailed observations, identifying and controlling variables, and creating an experiment to test his or her ideas.
- Suggest causes for what was observed.

Content

Student was able to:
- Explain that light bends when it passes through mediums with different densities; refraction of light is the bending of light.
- Infer that: The speed of light changes as it passes into different mediums or substances with different densities. When a pencil is put into a glass of water, the pencil looks broken, because as the light moves from the air through the glass and the water, it slows down.

2 points

Processes

Student was able to:
- Design an investigation to show what happens when light goes through the lens, including some observations, identifying and controlling some variables, and creating an experiment to test his or her ideas.
- Suggest causes for what was observed.

Content

Student was able to:
- Explain that light bends when it passes through water.
- Infer that: The light changes as it passes into a different medium or substance. When a pencil is put into a glass of water, the pencil looks broken, because as the light moves from the air through the glass and the water, it slows down.

1 point

Processes

Student was able to:
- Design an investigation to show what happens when light goes through the lens, including the creation of an experiment to test his or her ideas.
- Suggest causes for what was observed.

Content

Student was able to:
- Determine that something happens to the light when it passes through water. Student was able to infer that: The light changes as it passes into a different substance. When a pencil is put into a glass of water, the pencil looks broken, because as the light moves from the air through the glass and the water, it slows down.

Name: _____ Date: _____

STUDENT INQUIRY ACTIVITY **6** : WHAT DETERMINES HOW BRIGHT A LIGHT IS?

Topic: Brightness or Intensity

National Standards:
    NSES Unifying Concepts and Processes, (A), (B), (F), (G)
    NCTM Number and Operations, Measurement, Data Analysis and Probability

See **National Standards** section for more information on each standard.

Naive Concepts:
- Light from a bulb only extends outward a certain distance, and then stops. How far it extends depends on the brightness of the bulb.
- The effects of light are instantaneous. Light does not travel with a finite speed.
  (American Institute of Physics, 2000)

Materials:
2 different light sources (i.e., flashlight, burning incense, floodlight)
Meter stick
White button
Long room or hallway with little or no light when the lights are off

Science Skills: In this activity, students will be: **observing** the effects of varying the distance between a source of light and the viewer and using different sources of light. They will be **using numbers to measure** the distance between the source and the viewer, and **inferring** from their observations about the brightness or intensity of light in relation to the distance and the light source. Students will be **communicating** with each other while they are **manipulating materials**, **recording** and **interpreting data**, and **experimenting**.

Content Background:
Light travels in straight lines from its source and can change matter. Historically, there have been two theories as to how light travels. The **particle theory** suggests that light is made of particles, and the **wave theory** suggests it is made of waves. Newton proposed that light consists of particles that travel in straight lines through space. In 1900, Max Planck proposed that radiant energy comes in little bundles called **quanta**, later called **photons**. His theory helped other scientists understand that light behaves both as particles and waves, and helped to develop the theory of **Quantum Mechanics**. In 1905, Einstein's theory of photoelectric effect suggested that light consisted of bundles of concentrated electromagnetic energy that have no mass (photons). Current thought is that light travels in bundles of energy called photons that are emitted and absorbed as particles, but they travel as waves.

In 1880, Albert Michelson, an American physicist, conducted an experiment to determine the speed of light. We now know that the speed of light in a vacuum is a universal constant. This means that the electromagnetic spectrum of light can travel through a vacuum (i.e., through

53

Name: _____ Date: _____

STUDENT INQUIRY ACTIVITY **6**: WHAT DETERMINES HOW BRIGHT A LIGHT IS? (CONT.)

space) at the same speed. Light travels 186,000 miles per second (300,000 kilometers per second).

Brightness or intensity of light depends on the distance and the brightness of the source. Light intensity decreases by the square of the distance: the *Inverse Square Law*. For example, if the distance from the light source was 2 m, the intensity of the light would be 1/4 of the strength.

Challenge Question: What determines the brightness of a light source?

Procedure:

1. Examine the two different light sources. In the light source column of the data table, describe what each source is and any markings, such as the number of watts or volts on the source. In the brightness or intensity column, describe the differences in the amount of energy given off by each of the sources.

Light Source	Brightness or Intensity

2. Predict how large the source will look and how bright the light will look if it is farther away.

_____

_____

Exploration/Data Collection:

What determines the brightness of a light source?

Part I
Leave the room lights on.
1. Turn on the first light source.
2. Put the light source one meter away from you.
3. In the data table on the next page, describe the brightness or intensity of the light.
4. Put the light three meters away.

Name: _____ Date: _____

STUDENT INQUIRY ACTIVITY 6: WHAT DETERMINES HOW BRIGHT A LIGHT IS? (CONT.)

5. In the data table below, describe the brightness or intensity of the light.
6. Put the light five meters away.
7. In the data table below, describe the brightness or intensity of the light.
8. If your room is large enough, put the light ten meters away.
9. Record your data in the data table below.

Leave the room lights on.

10. Turn on the second light source.
11. Repeat steps 2–9.

LIGHT SOURCE DISTANCE VS. BRIGHTNESS *(Part I)*			
Light Source	**Distance (m)**	**Room Lights (off/on)**	**Brightness of Light**
	1 m		
	3 m		
	5 m		
	10 m		
	1 m		
	3 m		
	5 m		
	10 m		

Part II

Turn the light off in the room.

1. Turn on the first light source.
2. Put the light source one meter away from you.
3. In the data table on the next page, describe the brightness or intensity of the light.
4. Put the light three meters away.
5. In the data table on the next page, describe the brightness or intensity of the light.
6. Put the light five meters away.
7. In the data table on the next page, describe the brightness or intensity of the light.
8. If your room is large enough, put the light ten meters away.
9. Record your data in the data table on the next page.

Name: _____ Date: _____

STUDENT INQUIRY ACTIVITY 6: WHAT DETERMINES HOW BRIGHT A LIGHT IS? (CONT.)

Keep the lights in the room off.
10. Turn on the second light source.
11. Repeat steps 1–9.

LIGHT SOURCE DISTANCE VS. BRIGHTNESS *(Part II)*			
Light Source	**Distance (m)**	**Room Lights (off/on)**	**Brightness of Light**
	1 m		
	3 m		
	5 m		
	10 m		
	1 m		
	3 m		
	5 m		
	10 m		

1. When the light is on, what happens to the brightness or the intensity of each light source as it gets farther away? Explain how you know.

_____

_____

_____

_____

2. When the light is off, what happens to the brightness or intensity of each light source as you get farther away? Explain how you know.

_____

_____

_____

56

Name: _____   Date: _____

STUDENT INQUIRY ACTIVITY **6**: WHAT DETERMINES HOW BRIGHT A LIGHT IS? (CONT.)

3. What factors determine the brightness of a light?

_____

_____

_____

Summary:
    The brightness or intensity of the light depends on the distance and amount of energy coming from the light source. For example, stars look like they are tiny pinpoints of light, when in reality, they are anywhere from 10 to 865,000,000 miles in diameter. A 50-watt bulb is not as bright as a 100-watt bulb. According to the Inverse Square Law, a quantity varies inversely as another quantity is squared. Light intensity decreases by the square of the distance. For example, if the distance is 2 m, the brightness or intensity will be 1/4 of the brightness that it had at the light source.

Real-World Application:
    The brightness or intensity of light is used in photography. Light meters in cameras are used to determine if there is enough light to take pictures.
    There are over 200 billion billion stars in the sky. They are enormous; the largest stars are 1,000 times the diameter of our sun. The sun is 865,000 miles in diameter and is considered a medium-sized star. Neutron stars are the smallest; they are about ten miles in diameter. The brightness of the stars depends on the distance from the viewer, size, and amount of light given off.

Integration:
    This light activity can be integrated into earth science and astronomy, bringing in the brightness, size, and location of the stars. Mathematics is integrated through the measurement of the distances and data collection and analysis.

Extensions:
    One extension could be to conduct an investigation to determine the difference between a light source and reflected light and the difference between the reflected light and the light source in light and dark rooms. Mathematical determination of the intensity of light calculated with the *Inverse Square Law* formula could also be an extension.

Light and Color   Student Inquiry Activity 6: What Determines How Bright a Light Is?

Name: _____ Date: _____

STUDENT INQUIRY ACTIVITY 6: WHAT DETERMINES HOW BRIGHT A LIGHT IS? (CONT.)

Activity Assessment:

Directions: Award points for the level of mastery of the student.

3 points

Student was able to explain:
- That the relationship of distance from the source and brightness or intensity of the light source decreases the farther away the light source is.
- There was a difference in the amount of energy given off in the two different sources.
- That the relationship of the amount of energy of the source and the brightness or intensity of the light source depends on the amount of energy the light source gives out.
- These two things: that the distance from the viewer and the amount of energy the light source has affects the light brightness or intensity.

2 points

Student was able to explain:
- That there was a relationship between the distance from the source and the brightness or intensity of the light.
- There was a difference in the amount of energy given off in the two different sources.
- That there was a relationship between the amount of energy of the source and the brightness or intensity of the light.
- One of these two things: that the distance from the viewer affects the light brightness or intensity, or the amount of energy the light source has affects the light brightness or intensity.

1 point

Student was able to:
- Explain that there was a difference in the light sources.
- Explain that there was a difference as the light moved away.
- Make some conclusions.

Name: _____ Date: _____

STUDENT INQUIRY ACTIVITY **7** : LIGHT BREAKING APART AND GETTING BACK TOGETHER

Topic: Prisms/Color Wheels

National Standards:
   NSES Unifying Concepts, (A), (B), (E)
   NCTM Data Analysis

See **National Standards** sections for more information on each standard.

Naive Concepts:
* A white light source, such as an incandescent or fluorescent bulb, produces light made up of only one color.
* Sunlight is different from other sources of light because it contains no color.
* When white light passes through a prism, color is added to the light.
* The primary colors for mixing colored lights are red, blue, and yellow.
* A colored light striking an object produces a shadow behind it that is the same color as the light. For example, when red light strikes an object, a red shadow is formed.
* When white light passes through a colored filter, the filter adds color to the light.
* White light is colorless and clear, enabling you to see the "true" color of an object.
* When a colored light illuminates a colored object, the color of the light mixes with the color of the object.
   (American Institute of Physics, 2000)

Materials:
White paper
Empty clear glass or plastic bottle (i.e., syrup bottle)
Clear bottle of clear hand soap
Light source (i.e., bright flashlight)
White index card (or other white cardboard)
Crayons
String
5" x 8" unlined index card

Sink
Suncatcher, if available
Protractor

   Science Skills: Students will be **manipulating** materials to **conduct an experiment** to show that white light is made up of many colors. During this activity, students are **observing** what happens when light passes through a prism and when a color wheel spins, and they are **predicting** what happens when light passes through a prism. They will be **inferring** why it divides the white light into colors and why the colors on the color wheel seem to blend together. During the activity, students will be **communicating** and **developing vocabulary** related to refraction and persistent vision. Students will be **measuring** the angles of the bottles.

Name: _____ Date: _____

STUDENT INQUIRY ACTIVITY 7 : LIGHT BREAKING APART AND GETTING BACK TOGETHER (CONT.)

Content Background:

White light is made up of many colors. If white light strikes an object, it may absorb or reflect any or all of the parts of the color spectrum. That is why we see different colors. We see a red shirt, because only red light is reflected off the shirt; all other colors of the spectrum making up white light are absorbed. White objects reflect all colors; black objects absorb all colors.

A prism separates light into the colors of the visible spectrum. (You can remember the order of the colors in the visible spectrum with the acronym ROY G. BIV—red, orange, yellow, green, blue, indigo, violet.) The separation of light by its frequency is called **dispersion**. Different colors of light have different frequencies. As the light enters at an angle and passes through the prism, it slows down and is bent, once going in and once going out of the prism. Since the speed of light changes, so does the frequency.

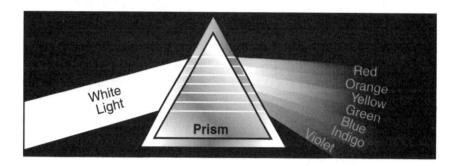

A prism disperses white light, and a color wheel can put all of the colors of the visible spectrum back together again. A color wheel has pie-shaped sections colored with the colors of the visible spectrum, and it is spun around. When the wheel spins fast enough that the individual colors in the wheel are held by the retina for a short period of time, the colors blend to make the wheel look white.

When different colors of light are mixed, they are **additive**. When the color filters are combined on a white screen, they produce different colors. When two complementary colors of light are added together on the white screen, they make white light. The complementary colors of light are blue and yellow, green and magenta, and red and cyan.

Lingering images (persistent vision) can illustrate complementary colors of light. If you stared at a brightly colored piece of paper, and then a white piece of paper, the complementary color will appear on the white paper. This is a result of the eye becoming tired of staring at the color, so you see the complementary color. Another example of persistent vision is the gerbil in the cage activity. In this activity, the gerbil appears to be inside the cage, even though one image is on one side of the card, and one image is on the other side of the card.

Name: _____   Date: _____

STUDENT INQUIRY ACTIVITY 7 : LIGHT BREAKING APART AND G. BACK TOGETHER (CONT.)

Challenge Questions:

How can white light be separated into the colors of the visible spectrum?

How can the colors of the visible spectrum be made into white light?

Procedure:

1. Fill the empty clear glass or plastic bottle two-thirds full of clear soap, and tighten the cap.
2. Tip the bottle over the sink so it is at an angle.
3. Shine a flashlight through the bottom edge of the bottle, and project it on a white ceiling or other white surface.
4. Try shining the light through the bottle at different angles.
5. Using a protractor, measure the angle of the bottle.

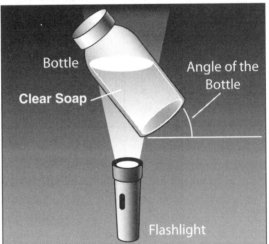

6. Describe what you see.

_____

_____

_____

7. What is causing what you see?

_____

_____

_____

.ame: _____ Date: _____

STUDENT INQUIRY ACTIVITY 7 : LIGHT BREAKING APART AND GETTING BACK TOGETHER (CONT.)

Exploration/Data Collection:
Part I

8. Be sure the cap is tight on the soap bottle.

9. Shine the light through the bottle at different angles onto a white surface.

10. Describe what you see.

    _____

    _____

    _____

Bottle	Angle of the Bottle	Draw What You See

11. What is causing what you see?

    _____

    _____

    _____

12. What makes up white light?

    _____

    _____

    _____

Name: _____ Date: _____

STUDENT INQUIRY ACTIVITY **7** : LIGHT BREAKING APART AND GETTING BACK TOGETHER (CONT.)

Part II
Color Wheel

1. Using the pattern below, construct a color wheel.
2. Trace the pattern on an unlined index card and color it according to the color code.
3. Poke two holes where the black dots are on the pattern.
4. Make a loop of string and put it through the holes. See diagram below.

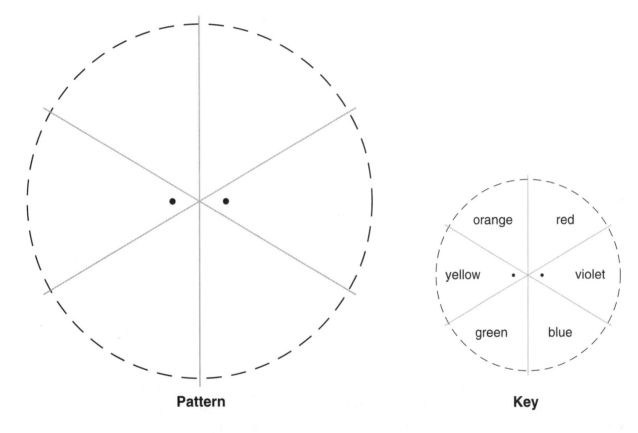

Pattern   **Key**

5. Wind up the string by flipping the wheel over, like you were turning a jumprope.
6. Place your fingers inside the loop, and spread out the strings. The wheel should start spinning.

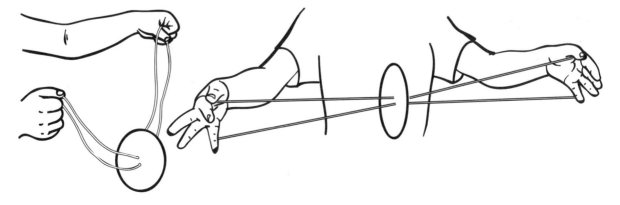

63

Name: _____   Date: _____

STUDENT INQUIRY ACTIVITY 7 : LIGHT BREAKING APART AND GETTING BACK TOGETHER (CONT.)

7. What do you see when you spin the color wheel?

_____

_____

_____

8. Based on what you learned about white light in Part I, explain why this happens.

_____

_____

_____

Summary:

White light is made up of many colors. If white light strikes an object, the object may absorb or reflect any or all of the parts of the color spectrum. The visible spectrum of colors is formed when the light passes through the soap bottle. When the light waves pass at an angle through the glass, plastic, or soap, it bends because of the different densities of the materials. The light bends once going into the bottles and again as it is coming out. Each color making up white light has a different frequency. Due to the varying thicknesses of the bottles and the liquids in them where the light passes, some will be bent more than others. The more dense the material is, the faster the light can travel through it. The light passing through the thickest part will be where the light speeds up the most and is bent the most; this will be the violet end of the color spectrum. The red will be where the liquid is thinnest, will speed up the least, and be bent the least. The colors in the visible spectrum are red, orange, yellow, green, blue, indigo, and violet (ROY G. BIV). A rainbow is produced because the falling raindrops act as tiny prisms.

When the color wheel spins, each color in the wheel is held by the retina of the eye for a short period of time (persistence of vision). If the disk spins fast enough, the colors blend to make white light.

Real-World Application:

Real-world applications of these topics are suncatchers, rainbows, the colors seen on CDs, etc.

Name: _____ Date: _____

STUDENT INQUIRY ACTIVITY 7 : LIGHT BREAKING APART AND GETTING BACK TOGETHER (CONT.)

Extensions:

One extension is to examine the effects of light on a CD. It looks as if it has multiple colors on it, because the laser cuts on it act as small prisms.

Lingering images can illustrate complementary colors of light. If you stare at a brightly colored piece of paper and then a white piece of paper, the complementary color will appear on the white paper. This is because the eye becomes tired of staring at the color, so you see the complementary color. Another example of persistent vision is the gerbil in the cage activity. In this activity, the gerbil appears to be inside the cage, even though one image is on one side of the card, and one image is on the other side of the card.

1. Create a gerbil and cage card on a string as you did with the color wheel.

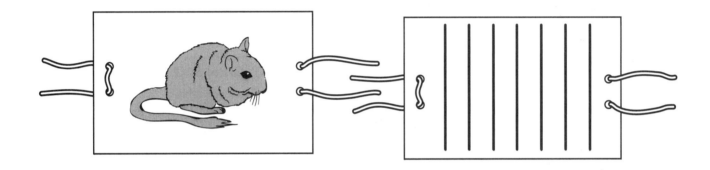

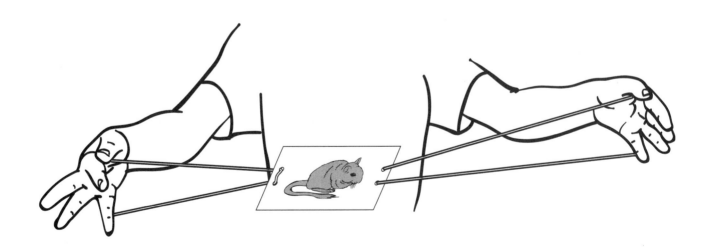

     65

Name: _____ Date: _____

STUDENT INQUIRY ACTIVITY 7 : LIGHT BREAKING APART AND GETTING BACK TOGETHER (CONT.)

Activity Assessment:

Directions: Award points based on the level of mastery by the student.

Part I			
4 points	**3 points**	**2 points**	**1 point**
White light is made up of many colors. When light passes through a substance more dense than air, it speeds up and bends. Colors making up white light have different frequencies. Violet has the highest frequency; red has the lowest. Different thicknesses of the bottles and liquids speed up the light at different rates, changing the frequency and separating into the colors that make it up. The colors of the visible spectrum are ROY G. BIV.	White light is made up of many colors. When light passes through a substance more dense than air, it speeds up and bends. Colors making up white light have different frequencies. Different thicknesses of the bottles and liquids speed up the light at different rates, changing the frequency and separating into the colors that make it up. The colors of the visible spectrum are ROY G. BIV.	White light is made up of many colors. When light passes through a substance more dense than air, the speed changes, and it bends. Different thicknesses of the bottles and liquids bend the light, making the colors that make it up. The colors of the visible spectrum are ROY G. BIV.	White light is made up of many colors. When light passes through a substance more dense than air, it bends.

Part II			
2 points	**1 point**		
Each color on the color wheel lingers in the retina, so if the wheel spins fast enough, the colors will all blend, and you will see white light.	When the color wheel spins, you will see white light.		

66

Name: _____ Date: _____

STUDENT INQUIRY ACTIVITY 8 : LIGHT ADDITION AND PIGMENT SUBTRACTION ACTIVITY

Topic: Mixing and Separating Pigments

National Standards:
  NSES Unifying Concepts and Processes, (A), (B), (F), (G)
  NCTM Data Analysis, Measurement

See **National Standards** section for more information on each standard.

Naive Concepts:
- The rules for mixing color paints and crayons are the same as the rules for mixing colored lights.
- The different colors appearing in colored pictures printed in magazines and newspapers are produced by using different inks with all of the corresponding colors.
- The mixing of colored paints and pigments follows the same rules as the mixing of colored lights.
- The primary colors used by artists (red, yellow, and blue) are the same as the primary colors for all color mixing.
- Color is a property of an object and is independent of both the illuminating light and the receiver (eye).
- The shades of gray in a black-and-white newspaper picture are produced by using inks with different shades of gray.

  (American Institute of Physics, 2000)

Materials:
Food coloring: red, blue, green, and yellow
Styrofoam™ egg carton
Toothpicks
Coffee filters (flat coffee filters used in 1–2 cup coffeemakers)
Black water-soluble markers
Large cup
Water

  Science Skills: Students will be **observing** color pigments, **using numbers** and **measuring** the volumes of water and food coloring. Students will be **inferring** what causes the difference between mixing pigments and colored lights. They will be **manipulating materials** to make **predictions, develop questions, identify** and **control variables,** and **conduct an experiment** to determine what happens when different colors are mixed. Students will be **communicating** and **developing vocabulary** during the process of **collecting, recording, analyzing,** and **interpreting data.**

Name: _____ Date: _____

STUDENT INQUIRY ACTIVITY 8 : LIGHT ADDITION AND PIGMENT SUBTRACTION ACTIVITY (CONT.)

Content Background:

When mixing pigments or paints, the colors are subtractive, instead of additive. When pigments are mixed, the colors are absorbed instead of being reflected. If blue and yellow pigments are mixed together, green is formed because green is the only color reflected. If red is mixed with green, the red absorbs the green, and the green absorbs the red, and the resulting mixture looks black. You will never get white when mixing color pigments. When more than two pigments are mixed, black is most likely created.

Using a process called **chromatography**, the colors can be separated. For example, when a mark is made on a coffee filter with a black, water-soluble marker and the edge of the filter is placed in water, the colors making up the black will separate. This happens because the inks are soluble in water, and different colors are more or less soluble, so you end up with a series of bands of colors. Scientists use this process to separate different materials.

Challenge Question: Are the results the same when you mix colored pigments and colored lights?

Procedure:

1. Predict what you think will happen if the colors of food coloring listed in the data table below are mixed. Use the egg carton cups to mix the colors to test your predictions.

Mixing Pigment Colors

Colors Mixed	Predictions	Results
Red + Blue		
Red + Yellow		
Red + Green		
Blue + Yellow		
Blue + Green		
Yellow + Green		

2. Were your predictions correct? _____

_____

_____

Name: _____ Date: _____

STUDENT INQUIRY ACTIVITY 8 : LIGHT ADDITION AND PIGMENT SUBTRACTION ACTIVITY (CONT.)

3. Would the number of drops make a difference in the colors you produced? Explain.

_____

_____

_____

4. Experiment and record your data.

Mixing Pigment Colors

Colors Mixed	Predictions	Results
Red + Blue		
Red + Yellow		
Red + Green		
Blue + Yellow		
Blue + Green		
Yellow + Green		

Exploration/Data Collection:
Chromatography

5. Using a black, water-soluble marker, make a black line on the bottom of the coffee filter. Put the bottom edge of the filter in 0.5 cm of water.

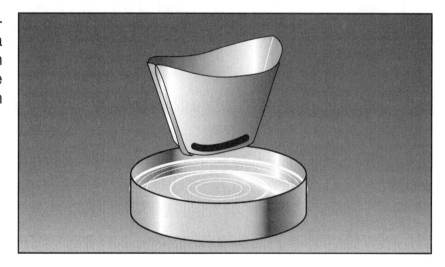

Name: _____ Date: _____

STUDENT INQUIRY ACTIVITY **8** : LIGHT ADDITION AND PIGMENT SUBTRACTION ACTIVITY (CONT.)

6. Describe what happens. _____

_____

_____

_____

7. Based on the data you collected in the Mixing Pigment Colors data table and the observations made, explain why you think this is happening.

_____

_____

_____

_____

_____

Summary:

When mixing pigments, the colors are **subtractive**. This means that when pigments are mixed, the colors are absorbed. If red is mixed with green, the red absorbs the green. When more than two pigments are mixed, black is most likely created. When the coffee filter is put into the water, the ink climbs up the filter, due to the capillary action. As the water climbs, the black ink is separated into the different colors of pigments making it up, because the ink is water-soluble. The order in which the colors separate is due to how soluble each color of ink is in water.

Real-World Application:

Mixing house paint or making different colors of ink are real-world examples of this activity.

Integration:

This lesson can easily be integrated with art and creating different colors by mixing the primary colors of pigments.

Extensions:

Try the exploration using green, purple, or brown water-soluble markers.

Name: _____ Date: _____

STUDENT INQUIRY ACTIVITY 9 : LIGHT AND COLOR ASSESSMENT ACTIVITY—HOW DO WE SEE?

Topic: Light and Life Science

National Standards:
    NSES Unifying Concepts and Processes, (A), (B), (C)
    NCTM Data Collection and Analysis

See **National Standards** section for more information on each standard.

Naive Concepts:
- The pupil of the eye is a black object or spot on the surface of the eye.
- The eye receives upright images.
- The lens is the only part of the eye responsible for focusing light.
- The lens forms an image (picture) on the retina. The brain then "looks" at this image and that is how we see.
- The eye is the only organ used for sight; the brain is used only for thinking.
  (American Institute of Physics, 2000)

Materials:
Eye drawing
Mirror
Pencil and paper

Science Skills: Students will be **observing** their eyes and the eyes of others **using numbers** and **measuring**. Students will be **inferring** how an eye uses light to work. They will be **manipulating materials** to make **predictions** and **conducting an experiment** to determine how the eye works. Students will be **communicating** and **developing vocabulary** while they are **collecting**, **recording**, **analyzing**, and **interpreting** data.

Content Background:
    When light strikes an object, it is reflected, absorbed, or passes through the object. Objects that allow all light to pass through are called **transparent**. **Translucent** objects allow some light to pass through, and **opaque** objects allow no light to pass through. Light colors reflect more light, and dark colors absorb more light.
    Lenses work because of refraction. Lenses are transparent objects with at least one curved surface. Double convex lenses are thicker in the middle and thinner on the edges, and light converges or comes together when it passes through the lens.
    White light is made up of many colors. If white light strikes an object, the object may absorb or reflect any or all of the parts of the color spectrum. That is why we see different colors. We see a red shirt, because only red light is reflected off of the shirt. All other colors of the spectrum making up white light are absorbed. White objects reflect all colors; black objects absorb all colors.

Name: _____ Date: _____

Student Inquiry Activity 9: Light and Color Assessment Activity—How Do We See? (cont.)

The inside of the eye consists of the cornea, iris, pupil, sclera, lens, and optic nerve. The outside of the eye has eyelids, eyelashes, and tear ducts that protect the inside of the eye.

Light strikes an object and is absorbed or reflected off it. The color of the object is determined by what colors are absorbed or reflected. The light travels to your **cornea**, a transparent material that acts like a convex lens. The light enters the interior of the eye through the pupil. The **pupil** is an opening in the center of the **iris**, or colored part of the eye. The iris has muscles that expand and contract the pupil. The pupil opens and closes, depending on how much light is available. If there is very little light, it opens wider, and if there is a lot of light, it becomes very small. The light passes through the pupil to another convex **lens**. As the light passes through the cornea and the lens, it is refracted or bent. These lenses focus the light on the back of the eye or retina. Between the lens and the retina is the **vitreous humor**, a transparent jelly of salts and proteins encased in the **sclera**, the white part of the eye. The **retina** is a tissue of light-sensitive cells that absorbs light rays and changes them to electrical signals. Due to the refraction caused by the convex lenses, the image on the retina is upside-down. The retina changes the light rays into electrical signals that are sent through the **optic nerve** to the brain, where what you are seeing is identified.

Challenge Question: How do we see?

Procedure:

1. Use the mirror to examine your eye.

2. Describe what you see.

   _____

   _____

   _____

   _____

3. Describe how you think your eye works.

   _____

   _____

   _____

   _____

Name: _____ Date: _____

STUDENT INQUIRY ACTIVITY 9: LIGHT AND COLOR ASSESSMENT ACTIVITY—HOW DO WE SEE? (CONT.)

Exploration/Data Collection:

4. While you are looking in the mirror, have someone turn off the room lights.

5. Describe the change you see in your eyes.

   _____

   _____

   _____

   _____

6. While you are looking in the mirror, have someone turn the room lights back on.

7. Describe the change you see in your eyes when the lights first come on.

   _____

   _____

   _____

   _____

8. Wait a few seconds, and then describe the change in your eyes.

   _____

   _____

   _____

   _____

9. What is the black part of your eye called? _____

   _____

Name: _____   Date: _____

STUDENT INQUIRY ACTIVITY 9: LIGHT AND COLOR ASSESSMENT ACTIVITY—HOW DO WE SEE? (CONT.)

10. Examine the drawing of the eye below. Describe how the eye works, starting from when the light hits the object and continuing until it goes to your brain to identify objects you are seeing via the optic nerve.

_____

_____

_____

_____

_____

The Human Eye

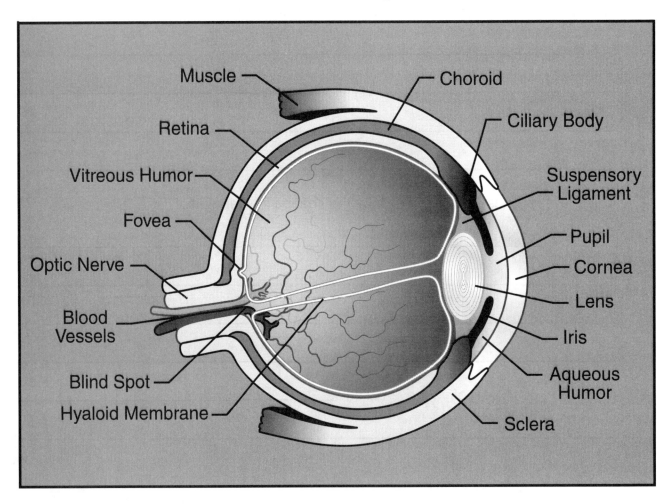

Name: _____ Date: _____

STUDENT INQUIRY ACTIVITY 9: LIGHT AND COLOR ASSESSMENT ACTIVITY—HOW DO WE SEE? (CONT.)

Summary:

The inside of the eye consists of the cornea, iris, pupil, sclera, lens, and optic nerve. The outside of the eye has eyelids, eyelashes, and tear ducts that protect the inside of the eye.

The light hits the object and reflects off it. The color of the object is determined by what colors are absorbed or reflected. For example, a red object will reflect red and absorb all of the rest of the colors in the visible spectrum. The light travels to your cornea. The cornea is a transparent material that acts like a convex lens. The light enters the interior of the eye through the pupil. The pupil is an opening in the center of the iris, or colored part of the eye. The iris has muscles that expand and contract the pupil. The pupil opens and closes, depending on how much light is available. If there is very little light, it opens wider; if there is a lot of light, it becomes very small. The light passes through the pupil to another convex lens. Lenses are transparent objects with at least one curved surface. As the light passes through the cornea and the lens, it is refracted or bent. These lenses focus the light on the back of the eye or retina. The retina is a tissue of light-sensitive cells that absorbs light rays and changes them to electrical signals. Between the lens and the retina is the vitreous humor, a transparent jelly of salts and proteins encased in the sclera, the white part of the eye. Due to the refraction caused by the convex lenses, the image on the retina is upside-down. When the retina changes the light rays into electrical signals, they are sent through the optic nerve to the brain, where what you are seeing is identified. Blood vessels in your eye bring food to the eye.

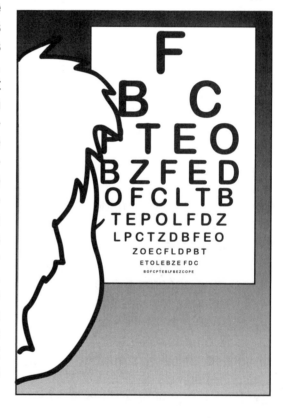

Real-World Application:

Making lenses to correct vision problems.

Integration:

This activity integrates the physics principles of light, including refraction, reflection, and conversion to another form.

Extensions:

An extension for this activity could be to examine different students' eyeglasses to determine if they are near- or farsighted.

75

Name: _____ Date: _____

STUDENT INQUIRY ACTIVITY 9: LIGHT AND COLOR ASSESSMENT ACTIVITY—HOW DO WE SEE? (CONT.)

Activity Assessment:

Directions: Rate student as exceptional, acceptable, or unacceptable based on his or her mastery of the skills below.

Exceptional	Acceptable	Unacceptable
Correctly uses and explains all of the characteristics of light learned in this section, including: reflection—light bouncing off a surface; refraction—the bending of light; lenses—transparent objects with at least one curved surface. How color is seen: natural light is made up of the colors ROY G. BIV. Light strikes the object, reflects the color of the object, and absorbs the rest. A convex lens focuses the light. When light strikes an object, some is reflected, absorbed, or passes through.	Correctly uses and explains half of the characteristics of light learned in this section, including: reflection—light bouncing off a surface; refraction—the bending of light; lenses—transparent objects with at least one curved surface. How color is seen: natural light is made up of the colors ROY G. BIV. Light strikes the object, reflects the color of the object, and absorbs the rest. A convex lens focuses the light. When light strikes an object, some is reflected, absorbed, or passes through.	Correctly uses and explains one characteristic of light learned in this section, including: reflection—light bouncing off a surface; refraction—the bending of light; lenses—transparent objects with at least one curved surface. How color is seen: natural light is made up of the colors ROY G. BIV. Light strikes the object, reflects the color of the object, and absorbs the rest. A convex lens focuses the light. When light strikes an object, some is reflected, absorbed, or passes through.
Explains in detail how the eye works, including all of the following: Light strikes an object and is reflected; light travels to the eye in this order: cornea, pupil that is controlled by the iris, lens, and vitreous humor, then to the retina, where the light is converted to electrical charges that are sent via the optic nerve to the brain.	Explains in detail how the eye works, including some of the following: light strikes an object and is reflected; light travels to the eye in this order: cornea, pupil that is controlled by the iris, lens, and vitreous humor, then to the retina, where the light is converted to electrical charges that are sent via the optic nerve to the brain.	Explains that the light travels from the object to the eye, where the eye sees it.

BIBLIOGRAPHY

Curriculum Resources

Abruscato, J., Hassard, J. (1977). *The Whole Cosmos.* Glenview, IL: Scott, Foresman, and Co.

AIMS Education Foundation (1990). *Primarily Physics: Investigations in Sound, Light, and Heat Energy.* Fresno, CA: AIMS Education Foundation.

AIMS Education Foundation (1997). *Soap Bubbles and Films.* Fresno, CA: AIMS Education Foundation.

American Institute of Physics (Circa 1988). *Operation Physics: Behavior of Light.* American Institute of Physics.

American Institute of Physics (Circa 1988). *Operation Physics: Color and Vision.* American Institute of Physics.

American Institute of Physics (2000). *Children's Misconceptions About Science.* American Institute of Physics. Available online at: http://www.amasci.com/miscon/opphys.html.

Barber, J. (1986) *Bubbleology.* Berkeley, CA: GEMS Lawrence Hall of Science.

DiSpezio, M. (1999). *Optical Illusion Magic: Visual Tricks and Amusements.* New York, NY: Sterling Publicating Co., Inc.

DiSpezio, M. (2001). *Eye-popping Optical Illusions.* New York, NY: Sterling Publicating Co., Inc.

Education Development Center, Inc (1971). *ESS: Optics.* Hudson, NH: Delta Education.

Education Development Center, Inc (1968). *ESS: Mirror Cards.* Hudson, NH: Delta Education.

Feldman, A., Ford, P. (1989). *Scientists and Inventors: The People Who Made Technology From Earliest Times to Present.* London: Godrey Cave Associates Limited.

Gertz, S., Portman, D., Sarquis, M. (1996). *Teaching Physical Science Through Children's Literature.* Middletown, OH: Terrific Science Press.

Gunderson, P.E. (1999). *The Handy Physics Answer Book.* Farmington Hills, MI: Visible Ink Press.

Hewitt, P., Suchocki, J., Hewitt, L. (1999). *Conceptual Physical Science.* Menlo Park, CA: Addison Wesley Longman.

Hewitt, P., (1998). *Conceptual Physics.* Menlo Park, CA: Addison Wesley Longman.

Hewitt, P., (1999). *Conceptual Physics: The High School Physics Program.* Menlo Park, CA: Addison Wesley Longman.

Hellemans, A., Bunch, B. (1988). *The Timetables of Science: A Chronology of the Most Important People and Events in the History of Science.* New York, NY: Simon and Schuster.

Kent, A., Ward, A. (1983). *Introduction to Physics.* London, England: Usborne Publishing.

Liem, T. (1992). *Invitations to Science Inquiry: Over 400 Discrepant Events to Interest and Motivate Your Students into Learning Science.* Chion Hills, CA: Science Inquiry Enterprises.

Lorbeer, G. (2000). *Science Activities for Middle School Students.* Boston, MA: McGraw Hill.

Maestro, B. (2000). *The Story of Clocks and Calendars: Marking a Millennium.* New York, NY: Lothrop, Lee and Shepard Books.

Marson, R. (1991). *TOPS Learning Systems: Light—36 Task Card Activities.* Canby, OR: TOPS Learning Systems.

Myring, L., Kimmitt, M. (1984). *Usborne New Technology: Lasers—What They Can Do and How They Work.* Tulsa, OK: EDC Publishing.

National Learning Center (1994). *Delta Science Module: Color and Light.* Hudson, NH: Delta Education, Inc.

National Learning Center (1994). *Delta Science Module: Lenses and Mirrors.* Hudson, NH: Delta Education, Inc.

BIBLIOGRAPHY (CONT.)

Rogers, K., Howell, L., et. al. (2000). *The Usborne Internet-linked Science Encyclopedia.* London, England: Usborne Publishing Ltd.

Silverstein, S. (1981). *Light in the Attic.* New York, NY: Harper and Row.

Smith, A. (ed). (1996). *Usborne Big Book of Experiments.* Tulsa, OK: EDC Publishing.

Sneider, C., Gould, A., Hawthorne, C. (1993). *Color Analyzers.* Berkeley, CA: GEMS Lawrence Hall of Science.

Stevenson, R. L. (1998). *A Child's Garden of Verses.* New York, NY: William Morrow Publishing.

Taylor, B. (1998). *Teaching Energy With Toys: Complete Lessons for Grades 4–8.* Middletown, OH: Terrific Science Press.

Taylor, B., Poth, J., Portman, D. (1995). *Teaching Physics With Toys: Activities for Grades K–9.* Middletown, Ohio: Terrific Science Press.

Thiessen, R., Hillen, J., et. al. (2000). *Rays Reflections.* Fresno, CA: AIMS Education Foundation.

University of Toronto (1998). *References for Misconceptions in Chemistry.* Available online at: http://www.oise.utoronto.ca/~science/chemmisc.html

Williams, T. (1987). *The History of Invention: From Stone Axes to Silicon Chips.* New York, NY: Facts on File Publications.

Software

Dorling Kindersley (1995). *Encyclopedia of Science.* New York, NY: Dorling Kindersley Multimedia.

Stranger, D. (pub). (1998). *Thinkin' Science Series: ZAP!.* Redmond, WA: Edmark Corporation.

Websites

http://www.fi.edu/color/

http://www.exploratorium.edu/lightwalk/index.html

http://www.exploratorium.edu/lightwalk/lwinternet.html

http://www.tooter4kids.com/LightColor/LightandColorindex.htm

http://www.exploratorium.edu/scienceexplorer/picturesfrom_light.html

http://www.exploratorium.edu/scienceexplorer/sunclock.html

http://www.uen.org/cgi-bin/websql/lessons/l4.hts?id=7644&core=3

http://www.pbs.org/wgbh/nova/einstein/

http://www.iit.edu/~smile/ph9307.html

http://www.educ.uvic.ca/Faculty/sockenden/edb363/1999/projects/LightOptics/lessons.html

http://www.fi.edu/fellows/fellow7/mar99/light/index.shtml

http://www.thinkquest.org/library/lib/sitesumoutside.html?tname=13405&url=13405/intro/what.html

http://library.thinkquest.org/13405/intro/what.html

http://www.iit.edu/~smile/

http://plymouth.ces.state.nc.us/programs/behavior.html

http://www.fischer-tropsch.org/DOE/DOEreports/96209/96209toc.html

http://home.attbi.com/~slvaldez/hedrick/index.html

http://www.opticalres.com/kidoptx.html

http://www.ece.utexas.edu/projects/k12-fall98/14540/Group7/

http://quest.arc.nasa.gov/hst/QA/LightBehavior/index.html

http://www.canteach.ca/links/linklight.html

http://www.themosh.org/psd2002/athome/lessonone.asp

http://www.msnucleus.org/membership/html/k-6/as/physics/2/asp2.html